Science Projects About
Methods of Measuring

Robert Gardner

Science
Projects

Enslow Publishers, Inc.

40 Industrial Road   PO Box 38
Box 398   Aldershot
Berkeley Heights, NJ 07922   Hants GU12 6BP
USA   UK

http://www.enslow.com

Library of Congress Cataloging-in-Publication Data

Gardner, Robert, 1929–
    Science projects about methods of measuring / by Robert Gardner.
       p. cm. — (Science projects)
    Includes bibliographical references and index.
    Summary: Presents projects and experiments that involve measuring, covering such
topics as units of measure, accuracy, mass, measuring areas and volumes, temperature,
heat, times, speed, and indirect measurements.
    ISBN 0-7660-1169-0
    1. Mensuration—Experiments Juvenile literature. 2. Science projects Juvenile
literature. [1. Measurement—Experiments. 2. Experiments. 3. Science projects.]
I. Title. II. Series: Gardner, Robert, 1929–   Science projects.
QA465.G27   2000
530.8'076—dc21   99-35532
                                                  CIP
                                                     AC

Printed in the United States of America

10 9 8 7 6 5 4 3 2 1

To Our Readers:
All Internet addresses in this book were active and appropriate when we went to press. Any
comments or suggestions can be sent by e-mail to Comments @enslow.com or to the address
on the back cover.

Illustration Credits: Stephen F. Delisle

Cover Illustration: Jerry McCrea (foreground); © Corel Corporation
(background).

Contents

*appropriate ideas for science fair project

*appropriate ideas for science fair project

Introduction

Science is based on measurements, and if you want to do science, you must know how to measure things and be familiar with the units of measurement that scientists use. This book introduces you to measuring with projects and experiments that are enjoyable to do.

Most of the materials you will need can be found in your home or school. Several experiments may require materials that you can buy in a supermarket, a hobby or toy shop, or a hardware store. You will need someone to help you with a few activities that require more than one pair of hands. It would be best if you work with friends or adults who enjoy experimenting as much as you do. In that way you will all enjoy what you are doing. You will also need people to serve as subjects in several of the experiments.

There are warnings in the book to point out activities that could involve danger. In some cases, to avoid danger, you will be asked to work with an adult. Please do so. We do not want you to take any chances that could lead to an injury.

Like other good scientists, you will find it useful to record in a notebook your ideas, notes, data, and anything you can conclude from your experiments. By so doing, you can keep track of the information you gather and of the conclusions you reach. Using your notebook, you can refer to experiments you have done. That may help you in doing other projects. Because you will be making many calculations, you will find it helpful to have a pocket calculator nearby as you do these experiments and analyze the data you collect.

Today, physicists and chemists assume that matter is made up of atoms and molecules. There is good evidence for believing that atoms and molecules exist, but in this book we will simply assume their existence.

Science Fairs

Some projects in this book may be appropriate for a science fair. Those projects are indicated with an asterisk (*). However, judges at such fairs do not reward projects or experiments that are simply copied from a book. For example, plugging numbers into a formula you do not understand will not impress judges. A graph of data based on careful measurements you have made and used to find a relationship between two variables would be more likely to receive serious consideration.

Science fair judges tend to reward creative thought and imagination. It is difficult to be creative or imaginative unless you are really interested in your project. Consequently, be sure to choose a subject that appeals to you. And before you jump into a project, consider, too, your own talents and the cost of materials you will need.

If you decide to use a project from this book for a science fair, you should find ways to modify or extend it. This should not be difficult because you will probably discover that as you do these projects, new ideas for experiments will come to mind. Such experiments could make excellent science fair projects, particularly because the ideas are your own and are interesting to you.

If you decide to enter a science fair and have never done so before, you should read some of the books listed in the "Further

Reading," as well as *Science Fair Projects — Planning, Presenting, Succeeding*, which is one of the books in this series. The books that deal specifically with science fairs will provide plenty of helpful hints and lots of useful information that will enable you to avoid the pitfalls that sometimes plague first-time entrants. You will learn how to prepare appealing reports that include charts and graphs, how to set up and display your work, how to present your project, and how to relate to judges and visitors.

Safety First

Most of the projects included in this book are perfectly safe. However, the following safety rules are well worth reading before you start any project.

1. Do any experiments or projects, whether from this book or of your own design, under the supervision of a science teacher or other knowledgeable adult.

2. Read all instructions carefully before proceeding with a project. If you have questions, check with your supervisor before going any further.

3. Maintain a serious attitude while conducting experiments. Fooling around can be dangerous to you and to others.

4. Wear approved safety goggles when you are working with a flame or doing anything that might cause injury to your eyes.

5. Do not eat or drink while experimenting.

6. Have a first-aid kit nearby while you are experimenting.

7. Do not put your fingers or any object other than properly designed electrical connectors into electrical outlets.

8. Never experiment with household electricity except under the supervision of a knowledgeable adult.

9. Do not touch a lit high-wattage bulb. Lightbulbs produce not only light, but also heat.

10. Many substances are poisonous. Do not taste any substances unless instructed to do so.

11. Keep flammable materials such as alcohol away from flames and other sources of heat.

12. If a thermometer breaks, inform your adult supervisor. Do not touch either the mercury or the broken glass with your bare hands.

1

Measuring and Units of Measure

Without measurements and mathematics there would be no science. Galileo, the father of modern science, likened the universe to a grand book. He wrote,

> The book cannot be understood unless one first learns to comprehend the language and read the letters in which it is composed. [The universe] is written in the language of mathematics, and its characters are triangles, circles, and other geometric figures without which it is humanly impossible to understand a single word of it; without these, one wanders about in a dark labyrinth.

Nineteenth-century English physicist Lord Kelvin (William Thomson) once said, "When you can measure what you are speaking about, and express it in numbers, you know something about it." He went on to say, "When you cannot measure it, when you cannot express it in numbers, your knowledge is of a meager and unsatisfactory kind."

All measurements must be in units to have meaning. To say that a person is 5.5 is meaningless. We would all ask, "Five-point-five what?" How much more meaningful the numbers become when we say the person is 5.5 feet tall. We know immediately that he or she is 5 feet, 6 inches tall. Similarly, if a recipe calls for 2 flour, the cook immediately wants to know 2 what? Cups? Tablespoons? Liters? Pints?

An American automobile driver stopped for fuel in England. She was surprised when, after filling the car's tank with gasoline, the cost was far more than expected. The numbers beside the fuel pump read 0.60; consequently, the driver expected to spend about $6.00 to fill the tank with about 10 gallons of gasoline. When the tank was filled, the price meter read 24.00, and the fuel-dispensed meter read 40.00.

In most foreign countries, fuel is measured in liters, not gallons. One liter is about 1.06 quarts, and it takes 3.785 liters to equal one U.S. gallon. The driver had purchased 40 liters of fuel at £0.60 per liter, resulting in a total cost of £24.00. The cost in U.S. money was about $40. The English pound (£) was worth about $1.67 when the gasoline was purchased. Gasoline is very expensive in foreign countries because it is heavily taxed.

Although measurement is essential to science, the earliest measurements were not made by scientists. They were made by craftsmen who realized that they could not make things that fit well together without measuring. The need to measure is mentioned in the sixth chapter of the book of Genesis in the Bible. God tells Noah to build an ark 300 cubits long, 50 cubits wide, and 30 cubits high.

1-1
The First Units of Measure

The cubit, Noah's unit of length according to the Bible, is the length of a person's forearm, from the elbow to the tip of the middle finger. The world's first units of measure, such as cubits, were based on parts of the human body. Other body parts that were used as units of measure are listed below and shown in Figure 1.

Things you will need:

• a room you can measure

• an adult

• pencil

• roll of wrapping paper

• tape

• people, including adults, siblings, and friends

- The *foot* was a unit equal to the length of a person's foot, from the heel to the end of the big toe. It was about ⅔ of a cubit.

- The *thumb* was the width of a person's thumb. It was assumed to be 1/12 the length of a foot. The length of the top segment of the index finger was another unit equal in length to the width of the thumb.

- The *span* was the distance between the tips of the thumb and little finger when a person's fingers were spread as much as possible. The span was considered to be ½ cubit.

- The *hand* was the width of the back of a person's hand. It was assumed to be ½ span.

- The *yard* was the distance from a person's nose to the tip of the middle finger of his outstretched arm.

- The *fathom* was two yards—the distance between the two middle fingers when a person's arms were outstretched.

Make a table to show the relationships among these various units of measure. For example:

1 fathom = 2 yards = 4 cubits = 6 feet = 8 spans = 16 hands = 72 thumbs

1 yard = ? = ? = ? . . .

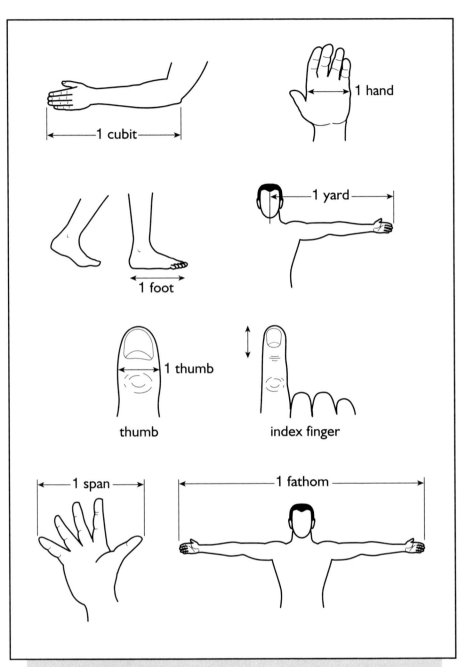

Figure 1. The earliest units of measure were based on body parts.

Measure the length and width of a room in your house, using your feet as a unit of length. What is the length of the room in feet? What is the width of the room in feet?

Next, have an adult take the same measurements. How do your measurements of the room compare with the adult's?

Use a pencil to mark the length of your cubit on a large sheet of wrapping paper. In the same way, mark the length of your foot, span, hand, and the width of your thumb. Tape a long sheet of the paper to a wall and mark the lengths of your yard and fathom.

Now determine whether or not your fathom is equal to two yards. Is your span equal to two hands? Is the length of the first segment of your index finger equal in length to the width of your thumb? Is your foot equal to 12 thumbs? Are two of your spans equal to your cubit? How does the length of your foot compare with the length of your cubit?

Compare the lengths of your cubit, foot, thumb, span, hand, yard, and fathom with those of other people. Include adults as well as siblings and friends. How do their units of measure compare with yours? What is the major problem in using body parts as units of measure?

1-2*
Your Own Measuring System

You can invent your own measuring system. Place a paper clip at one end of a long strip of thin cardboard, as shown in Figure 2a. Use a pencil to mark the length of the paper clip on the cardboard. You can give this

Things you will need:
- paper clip
- long strip of thin cardboard
- pencil
- scissors

length a name. You might call it a clip, or you can invent another name for it. Mark off nine more of these lengths end to end on the cardboard. Then use scissors to cut the cardboard so that it is exactly 10 paper clips long (Figure 2b). Give this length, equal to 10 paper clips, another name. You might assign it your surname in honor of you; you might call it a decaclip; you could name it with deca as a prefix to your surname; or call it *deca* plus whatever name you gave the length. *Deca* means "10 times," as in *decade* ("10 years").

Next, divide the smaller unit of length—the one equal to the length of a paper clip—into 10 equal divisions (Figure 2c). Give these small units of length a name as well. You might use the prefix deci, which means "one tenth" ($\frac{1}{10}$, or 0.1).

Using the prefixes in Table 1, develop additional units that are multiples or fractions of the paper clip that you used as your basic unit of length. Which of these units can you actually mark on the ruler you have made or on others you could make?

Exploring on Your Own

Design a system of measurement that uses the length of a coffee stirrer as its basic unit. Design another system that uses the width of a coffee stirrer as its basic unit.

You know the meaning of such prefixes as *milli-, centi-, deci-, deca-, hecto-,* and *kilo-*, but what do the prefixes *mega-, giga-, tera-, micro-, nano-,* and *pico-* indicate?

14

Table 1. Prefix names and numerical equivalents

Prefix	Meaning
milli-	0.001 ($\frac{1}{1,000}$)
centi-	0.01 ($\frac{1}{100}$)
deci-	0.10 ($\frac{1}{10}$)
deca-	10
hecto-	100
kilo-	1,000

Standard Units of Length

As you found in the previous experiment, units of measure based on body parts are not very useful. Your foot may be considerably shorter than an adult's and significantly longer than your little brother's or sister's. If you and an adult carpenter were to build a house, all the boards you measured and cut based on body measurements he made and requested might be too short. On the other hand, all the boards he measured and cut based on measurements you made and requested might be too long.

To avoid confusion and arguments in building and in the marketplace, Henry I, a twelfth-century English king, introduced the world's first standard unit of measure. Henry had an iron bar cut that was equal in length to the distance from his nose to the end of his outstretched arm. The bar, called the iron ulna, became the standard length for one yard. Copies of it could be made and used throughout the land. These copies eventually became the yardsticks so common in our homes. This standard length provided merchants and customers with an impartial and unchanging measure in matters related to length.

Later, another English king, Edward I, decreed that 1 yard would be equal to 3 feet. The foot, in turn, was divided into 12 equal segments. Each segment was defined as one inch. Consequently, a foot was the same length as 12 inches, and a yard was equal in length to 36 inches.

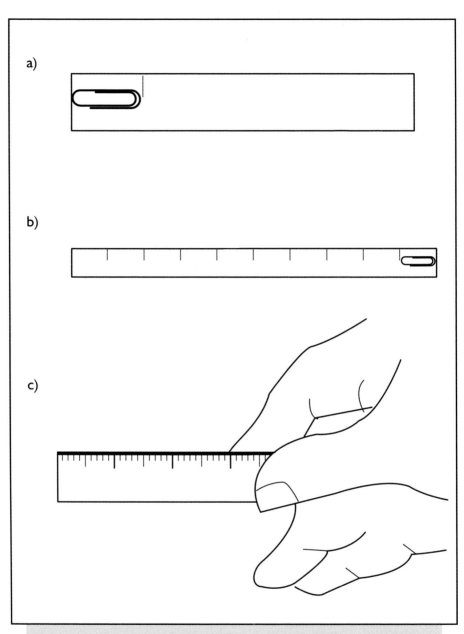

Figure 2. a) Mark the length of a paper clip on a cardboard strip. b) Repeat the process nine more times to make a length 10 paper clips long. c) Divide the paper clip lengths into 10 equal parts (deciclips).

The U.S. Customary System

The U.S. customary system of measurements had its origin in the old "body parts" system that was gradually standardized beginning with Henry I (King of England, 1068–1135). It is most widely used in the United States. As you can see from Table 2, the units are not related to one another in any mathematically simple or logical way.

Table 2: The U.S. Customary System of Linear Measurements

1 yard (yd) = 3 feet (ft) = 36 inches (in)
1 foot = 12 inches = $\frac{1}{3}$ yard
1 inch = $\frac{1}{12}$ foot = $\frac{1}{36}$ yard
1 rod = 16.5 feet = 5.5 yards
1 mile = 5,280 feet = 1,760 yards

The mile is a unit that was developed by the Romans. It was a distance equal to that of 1,000 paces by marching soldiers. (*Mille* means "one thousand" in Latin.) Since a pace, two steps, is about 5 feet, a mile was 5,000 feet. Today a mile is 5,280 feet.

The nautical mile, which is used by ships and planes, is based on a natural unit—the size of the earth. A nautical mile is equal to 1 minute of arc ($\frac{1}{60}$ of a degree) along the equator. Because the equator encircles the earth, it encompasses 360 degrees of arc.

The Metric System

Before the Revolution began in France in 1789, there were a number of different units of measure in that country, which led to confusion. Slowly, a new decimal system of weights and measures emerged.

But sometimes the overzealous government tried to establish reforms that the French people and the rest of the world refused to accept. For example, a new calendar consisted of 12 months, each with 30 days. To account for the additional days needed for the earth to make one orbit around the sun, the year concluded with a 5- or 6-day holiday. Each month was divided into three 10-day weeks. Each day was divided into ten 100-minute hours, and each minute contained 100 seconds.

Although the calendar and time systems were mathematically logical, they made it difficult to communicate with the rest of the world. The calendar was in effect for 12 years, but the decimal clock was never widely accepted.

The basic unit of length in the metric system is the meter (m). French scientists and mathematicians designed the meter to be one ten-millionth of the distance from the North Pole to the equator. To within less than 0.025 percent, a meter is one ten-millionth of the distance from the North Pole to the equator. In 1889 a standard meter bar with an X-shaped cross section to make it very rigid was made from an alloy of platinum and iridium. The distance between two lines engraved across the bar were used to establish the standard meter. Today the meter is more precisely defined as 1,650,763.73 wavelengths of a particular reddish-orange light emitted by an isotope (one kind of atom) of krypton.

Today's metric system is known as the International System of Units, or *Système International d'Unités*. It is more commonly referred to as SI in all languages, and it is managed by the International Bureau of Weights and Measures, whose headquarters are in Sèvres, France. In the United States, where U.S. customary units as well as metric are widely used, the National Bureau of Standards defines the yard as 3,600/3,937 m or 0.9144 m.

In addition to the meter, which is the world's standard length, SI also includes standard units for mass, time, temperature, electric current, light intensity, and amount of substance. You will encounter some of these units later in this book.

Table 3 gives the SI units of linear measure, which are based on the meter. As you can see, it is a decimal system. All the units are related to one another by a factor of 10 or $\frac{1}{10}$ (0.1).

Table 3: The SI System of Linear Measurement

1 meter (m) = 10 decimeters (dm)*
= 100 centimeters (cm)
=1,000 millimeters (mm)
1 dekameter (dam)* = 10 m
1 hectometer (hm)* = 100 m
1 kilometer (km) = 1,000 m
10 mm = 1 cm
10 cm = 1 dm
10 dm = 1 m
10 m = 1 dam
10 dam = 1 hm
10 hm = 1 km

*seldom used

1-3*
Metric Measure

If you are not familiar with SI (metric) units of length, a few minutes with a meterstick will help you see how simple and logical these units of measure are. If you do not have access to a meterstick, you can make one from a stick that is about 40 inches long. Place a 12-inch clear plastic ruler that also has metric units (centimeter and mil-

Things you will need:
- sharp pencil
- 1-foot clear plastic ruler marked with inches and centimeters
- paper
- various objects
- calculator
- yardstick
- meterstick or long stick and clear tape
- long piece of thin rope

limeter divisions) on it on the stick. Use the ruler and a pencil with soft lead to mark the 0- and 30-cm lines on the stick. Then use the same ruler to mark off centimeter divisions from 30 cm up to 100 cm. The centimeter marks are the longer numbered lines on the ruler. You need not mark the millimeter divisions, because you can use clear tape to fix the clear plastic ruler to the stick to cover the first 30 centimeters of your meterstick. That 30-cm portion of the meterstick can be used to take measurements that require millimeters.

Examine your meterstick closely. Notice that there are 100 centimeters in one meter. *Centi* means "one hundredth," so a centimeter is $\frac{1}{100}$ of a meter. Each centimeter is divided into 10 equal units called millimeters. *Milli* means "one thousandth," so a millimeter is $\frac{1}{1,000}$ of a meter. As you can see, there are 1,000 millimeters in a meter. Ten centimeters constitute a decimeter. *Deci* means "one tenth," so a decimeter is $\frac{1}{10}$ of a meter. There are 10 decimeters in a meter. If you used your meterstick to lay out a line 10 meters long, you would have a dekameter (*deka* means "ten"). If you laid 10 dekameter lengths end to end to make a length of 100 meters, you would have a hectometer (*hecto* means "one hundred"). And if you placed 10 hectometers end to end, you would have 10 times 100 meters or 1,000 meters, which is a kilometer (*kilo* means "one thousand").

Use your meterstick to measure a variety of objects such as this book; the length, width, and height of a room; your own height; and so on. To make use of millimeters, you could measure the width of a pencil or a piece of string.

Measure your height in centimeters or meters. If your height is 150 cm, what is your height in meters? In millimeters? In decimeters? Notice how easy it is to move from one SI unit to another. Think how much more difficult it would be to convert the same height—59 inches—to feet, yards, and rods.

Use a long piece of thin rope or thick string to make a measuring tape with a length of 1 dekameter. You can tie short pieces of colored yarn to your measuring tape at one-meter intervals. Use your measuring tape and meterstick to find the length and width of a soccer field. What other lengths would it be convenient to measure with such a measuring tape? How many times would you have to place your measuring tape on the ground to measure a length of 1.0 hectometer? To measure a kilometer?

Save your measuring tape and meterstick for measurements you may want to take later.

Exploring on Your Own

There are 60 minutes in each degree of arc. a) How long is the equator in nautical miles? b) A nautical mile is 1.152 miles. What is the earth's circumference as measured in miles?

The earth's circumference is 40,000,000 m. a) What is the earth's circumference in kilometers? b) What distance, in kilometers, is covered by one degree of arc along the equator? What is that distance in meters? c) What distance is covered by 1 minute of arc? d) There are 60 seconds in each minute of arc. The NAVSTAR global positioning system (GPS), which is a navigational system that uses several satellites and atomic clocks to determine location, can establish an object's position to within one second of arc. To within how many meters can the GPS determine a position on the earth?

Find out and explain how the NAVSTAR GPS works.

1-4*
Comparing Standard Units of Measure

As you know, rulers are used to measure length in both U.S. customary and SI units. Most commonly, rulers are divided into 12 inches or 30 centimeters or into 6 inches or 15 cm. Yardsticks, of course, are divided into 36 inches, and metersticks contain 100 cm. Each centimeter is divided into 10 millimeters, so there are 1,000 mm along the meterstick.

Things you will need:
- sharp pencil
- 1-foot ruler
- paper
- metric ruler
- calculator
- yardstick
- meterstick

In most countries, all measurements are made in SI units. In the United States, however, both SI and the U.S. customary units are in use. Carpenters and other craftspeople usually use the customary units. Scientists and a growing number of other people use SI units. As a result, it is often necessary to convert SI units to U.S. customary units or vice versa.

To find out how to make such conversions, make two marks exactly 10 inches apart on a sheet of paper, as shown in Figure 3. Next, use a metric ruler to find the distance between the two marks in centimeters. You will find that the distance is 25.4 cm.

If 25.4 cm is equal in length to 10 inches, how many centimeters equal 1 inch? Using a calculator, find the length of a centimeter in inches. What do you find it to be? How many centimeters are equal to one yard? What is the length of a yard in meters? What is the length of a foot in meters? In centimeters? What is the length of a meter in feet? How many meters are there in one mile? How many kilometers are equal to a mile? What is the length of one kilometer in miles?

Test as many of these conversions as you can directly by using metric and U.S. customary rulers, a yardstick, and a meterstick. Do your measurements appear to confirm the conversions you calculated? How do your conversions compare with those found in the Appendix?

Exploring on Your Own

In Experiment 1-2 you designed your own systems of measurement, using paper clips or coffee stirrers as your basic unit of measure. How can you convert the units in the systems you designed into U.S. customary or SI units of measure?

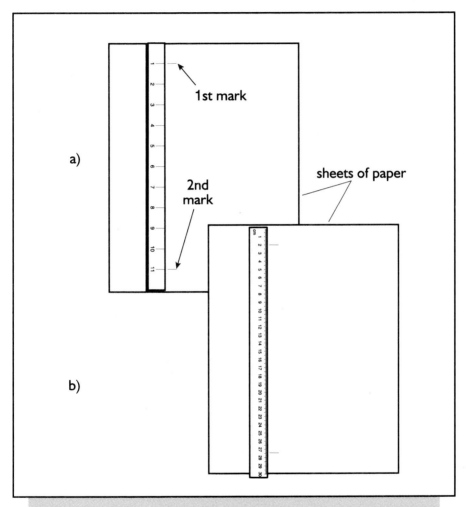

Figure 3. a) Make two marks exactly 10 inches apart, as shown. Do not use the end of the ruler: It may be worn. b) Use a metric ruler to find the distance in centimeters between the two marks.

1-5*
Converting Units Within and Between Measuring Systems

We sometimes have to convert units from SI to U.S. customary or within a system, from, say, kilometers to centimeters. This is easy to do if you use the

Things you will need:

• pencil

• paper

• calculator

factor-label method. This method involves using factors whose ratios are equal to one. As you know, multiplying by one does not change the value of a number, but it can change the units. For example, if you want to convert 2.5 km to meters, you can multiply 2.5 km by 1,000 m/km. The value of 1,000 m/1 km is 1, because 1 km is equal to 1,000 m. The actual calculation would look like this:

$$2.5 \text{ km} \times \frac{1,000 \text{ m}}{1 \text{ km}} = 2,500 \text{ m}$$

We strike through the km units because km/km also equals one, so they cancel. We have meters left, which is the unit we wanted. A unit divided by itself is 1, just as any value divided by itself is 1. For example, $\frac{2}{2}$, $\frac{3}{3}$, $\frac{4}{4}$, and so on are all equal to 1; similarly, cm/cm, m/m, ft/ft, yd/yd are also equal to 1.

To convert 1.6 km to centimeters, you could do the following:

$$1.6 \text{ km} \times \frac{1,000 \text{ m}}{1 \text{ km}} \times \frac{100 \text{ cm}}{1 \text{ m}} = 160,000 \text{ cm}$$

Both 1,000 m/1 km and 100 cm/1 m are equal to one, and the units km/km and m/m cancel, leaving cm as the unit.

Converting from U.S. customary units to SI units or vice versa involves the same principle. For example, you have found that 2.54 cm is the same length as 1 inch. If you want to convert 15 inches to centimeters, the process is the same.

$$15 \text{ in} \times \frac{2.54 \text{ cm}}{1 \text{ in}} = 38.1 \text{ cm}$$

The value of 2.54 cm/1 in is 1 because 2.54 cm is the same length as 1 in, and the unit inch divided by the unit inch is also 1. (You might say the units cancel.) That leaves centimeters as the unit for the number 38.1.

The factor-label method works both ways. If you want to convert 38.1 cm to inches, you would proceed in a similar way:

$$38.1 \text{ cm} \times \frac{1 \text{ in}}{2.54 \text{ cm}} = 15 \text{ in}$$

Or you could use the fact that one cm equals 0.3937 in and obtain the same result:

$$38.1 \text{ cm} \times \frac{0.3937 \text{ in}}{1 \text{ cm}} = 15 \text{ in}$$

The conversion factors in Table 4 will be useful when you have to change SI units to U.S. customary units or vice versa. SI units are predominant in this book because they are easier to use and because most scientific work uses SI units.

Table 4: Conversion factors

2.54 cm = 1.00 in
1.000 ft = 0.3048 m = 30.48 cm
1.000 yd = 0.9144 m
1.000 mile = 1.609 km
0.3937 in = 1.000 cm
1.000 m = 3.280 ft = 39.37 in
1.000 m = 1.094 yd
1.000 km = 0.6220 mi = 3,282ft = 1,094 yd

Exploring on Your Own

The length of a football field, excluding the goal areas, is 100 yards. Using the conversions in Table 4, calculate the length of a football field in meters. Then measure the field in meters. Does your measurement agree with your calculation?

Devise a way to determine the thickness of a sheet of paper.

At the equator, the earth's circumference is 40,000 kilometers. What is the circumference of the earth's line of latitude at 45 degrees north? At 60 degrees north? At the Arctic Circle? At the North Pole?

1-6*
Measuring Long Distances

You can measure long distances along the ground by placing metersticks or yardsticks end to end or by turning the same measuring stick end over end. But such a process is tedious. A much faster and easier way is to roll a wheel along the length you want to measure.

You can use a bicycle wheel to measure large distances. Mark a point on the circumference of the bicycle wheel with chalk or a marking pen. Make a similar mark on a playground or side-

walk, as shown in Figure 4a. The two marks should be even. Now roll the bike ahead slowly until the wheel has made one complete turn and the mark is again at the bottom of the wheel. Make a second mark on the playground or sidewalk. Again, the mark on the wheel and the mark on the ground should line up.

Now use a yardstick, meterstick, or ruler to measure the distance between the two marks on the ground. Each turn of the wheel measures a distance equal to the distance between the two lines you marked on the ground. To make each rotation of the wheel more visible, tie a short length of yarn to one of the spokes. How can you measure distance by counting the number of turns your bicycle wheel makes? **Do not try to ride your bike and count turns. It is much safer to walk and push your bike when you measure distances this way!**

You can make a trundle wheel that travels one meter for each turn. To do this, ask an adult to help you make a wooden disk that

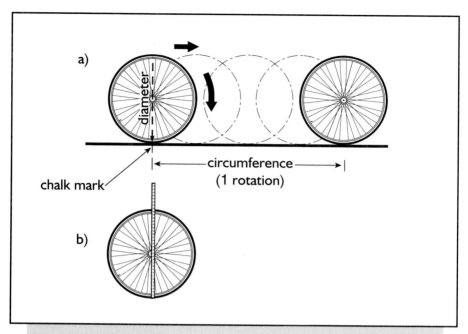

Figure 4. a) Roll the wheel through one revolution. Mark that distance—the wheel's circumference—on a sidewalk or driveway. What is the wheel's circumference? b) Using the same units, measure the wheel's diameter. What is the ratio of the wheel's circumference to its diameter?

is 32 cm (0.32 m) in diameter. If you measure the circumference of the disk (wheel), you will find that it is 1.00 m. How could you make a wheel that would travel 2.00 m per turn?

Ask the adult to help you drill a hole through the center of the disk. A long bolt through the hole can serve as an axle, as shown in Figure 5. The same figure shows how you can make a wooden handle about a meter long that can be connected to the wheel. How many times would a wheel with a diameter of 32 cm have to go around to travel one kilometer? To travel one mile?

Use your trundle wheel to measure the distance from your house to your school, playground, store, friend's house, or any other place you travel to frequently. **Remember to keep an eye on traffic when you are rolling the wheel.**

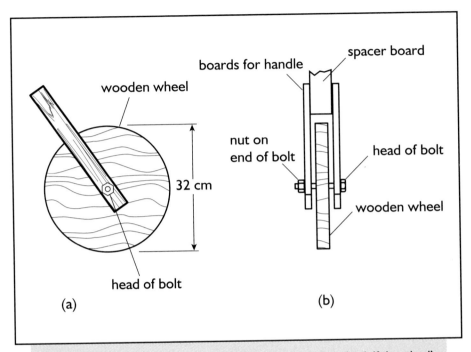

Figure 5. a) A side view of the wheel. b) A front view of the wheel. If the wheel's diameter is 32 cm, its circumference will be 1.00 m.

Another way to measure large distances is with paces. A geometric pace is the distance from the heel of one foot to the heel of the same foot in the next stride, as shown in Figure 6. Before you can measure distances in paces, you need to know the length of your pace. The best way to find this out is to mark a starting line. Beginning with your heel on the starting line, take 10 normal paces (20 steps), then mark an end line behind the same heel. Using a yardstick, meterstick, or measuring tape, find the distance between the two lines. How can you find the length of one of your paces?

Use geometric paces to measure the same distances you measured with your trundle wheel. How do the distances compare? Which device do you think is more accurate for measuring long distances? How can you determine which one is actually more accurate?

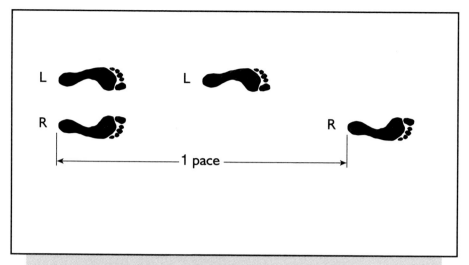

Figure 6. A geometric pace is measured from the heel of one foot to the heel of the same foot in the next stride. How long is your pace? For Roman soldiers it was about 5 feet.

Exploring on Your Own

Devise other methods to measure long distances on the earth.

Investigate how astronomers measure the distances to stars and planets.

1-7
Body Parts and Ratios

In 1975, a team of anthropologists led by Mary Leakey found two sets of footprints that were 3.5 million years old embedded in volcanic ash near Laetoli, Tanzania. They had been made by feet that were human in appearance—the footprints of our ancestors. The prints of the larger individual, perhaps a male, were 21.5 cm (8.5 in) long and about 47.2 cm (18.6 in) apart; the other set were 18.5 cm (7.3 in) long and 38.7 cm (15.2 in) apart. To determine the height of these upright creatures, the anthropologists assumed that a foot length is 15 percent (0.15) of an individual's height. What did they calculate the heights of these two creatures to be?

To see if their assumption was a reasonable one for present-day humans, you can conduct an experiment. Measure the foot length and the height of a number of different people. Try to include males and females of all ages. For each of the people you measure, determine the ratio of their foot length to their height. What is the average ratio of foot length to height for all the people you tested? Do your results for modern humans agree with the assumption made by the anthropologists about the human ancestors who made the footprints?

The ratio of foot length to height is but one of the many body-part ratios you might examine. Other ratios that you might try for a number of people include height to cubit, height to fathom, height to span, span to cubit, foot to cubit, length of small finger to length of nose, circumference of ankle to circumference of elbow, and any other body-part ratios you think may reveal a constant among a variety of people.

Do body-part ratios tend to be more constant among adults than among children?

Things you will need:

- ruler, meterstick, or yardstick
- many people of different ages, male and female
- pencil and paper
- calculator (optional)
- tape measure

1-8*
Circles, Diameters, and Circumferences

In the previous experiment, you learned how to use wheels to measure distances for which it would be inconvenient to use metersticks, yardsticks, or tape measures. In this experiment, you will look more closely at the relationship between a circle's diameter and its circumference.

To begin, you can repeat what you did with the bicycle wheel in Experiment 1-6. By marking the distance the wheel moves forward in one revolution, you have measured the wheel's circumference (the distance around the wheel), as shown in Figure 4a. Now, using the same units you used to measure the circumference, measure the wheel's diameter—the distance across the wheel's center (Figure 4b). Next, divide the wheel's circumference by its diameter to find the ratio: circumference/diameter. What is this ratio? The ratio will have no units because you are dividing meters by meters, centimeters by centimeters, feet by feet, or inches by inches.

Find as many circular objects as possible. In addition to wheels, you might use large coins, large tin cans, wastebaskets, drinking glasses, and so on. Measure the circumference and diameter of each circle and find their ratio. How closely do these ratios agree? Do you think the ratio of a circle's circumference to its diameter is a constant? If you do, what is the value of the constant?

Things you will need:

- bicycle
- chalk or marking pen
- playground or sidewalk
- yardstick, meterstick, ruler, or tape measure
- various circular objects such as large coins, tin cans, wastebaskets, drinking glasses, etc.
- calculator (optional)

Exploring on Your Own

How did scientists measure the diameter and circumference of the earth? Is the diameter of the earth from pole to pole the same as the diameter across its equator?

2

Measurement and Mass

As you know, measurements without units are meaningless, but even with units, they are never perfect. Measurements are comparisons between standard units of quantities such as meters or kilograms and the thing that is being measured. The instrument used to make a measurement is a copy of some standard such as the standard meter in Paris. The copy is not perfect, and the person making the measurement may be viewing the measuring instrument from an angle that distorts the reading. In the end, the person making a measurement has to estimate the final number on an instrument. Is it a little bit over the line? Under the line? Closer to 0.2 or 0.3 of the distance between two lines? Is it 1.25 cm or 1.26 cm? The actual measurement may be closer to 1.257 cm, but the person making the decision has to make the best estimate he or she can with the measuring instrument being used.

A measuring instrument may allow you to make precise measurements, which may not be very accurate. *Accurate* measurements are those that are very close to the true measurement. *Precise* measurements agree very closely with one another but may not be close to the true measurement. For example, a thermometer used by several different experimenters may show that water freezes at 1.005°C ± 0.001°C. This means that all the measurements are within one thousandth of a degree. This thermometer provides very precise measurements of temperature, because all the measurements are within one thousandth of a degree. Unfortunately, the thermometer does not provide accurate readings because the freezing temperature of water is 0.0°C, not a little more than 1.0°C.

Another thermometer might indicate that water freezes at 0.0°C ± 0.1°C. This thermometer is more accurate than the first, because the freezing temperature of water is 0°C and all the measurements on this thermometer are within one tenth of a degree of the true value. However, the second thermometer provides less precise measurements than the first because its readings vary by as much as one tenth of a degree, while measurements using the first thermometer agreed to within one thousandth of a degree.

Figure 7 uses a dartboard to illustrate accuracy and precision.

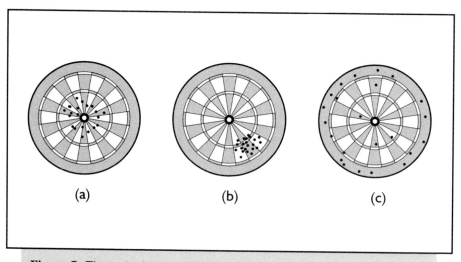

(a)   (b)   (c)

Figure 7. These dartboards illustrate the difference between accuracy and precision. a) The throws were accurate and precise. b) The throws were precise but not accurate. c) The throws were neither accurate nor precise.

2-1*
Improving the Accuracy of Measuring Small Objects

With care and a good ruler, you can estimate lengths to the nearest tenth of a millimeter (hundredths of a centimeter). You can make a simple device that will allow you to measure the diameter or width of very small objects more accurately than you

Things you will need:

• ruler
• sharp pencil
• index card
• shears or scissors
• small objects such as pencils, beads, wires, and string

can with a ruler. To measure hundredths and estimate thousandths of an inch, use a ruler and a sharp pencil to make two marks exactly 1 inch apart along the side of an index card, as shown in Figure 8a. Extend the lower mark horizontally across the card. This line is the base of a right triangle whose altitude is the one-inch interval along the edge of the card. Now place a metric ruler on the card to make the triangle's hypotenuse exactly 10 cm (100 mm) long. Draw the hypotenuse and use shears or scissors to carefully cut out the triangle, as shown in Figure 8b. Next, mark and number the ten 1-centimeter intervals along the hypotenuse. They should be labeled *0.1* to *1.0*. The 1.0 belongs, of course, at the wide edge of the triangle, where the side of the triangle had a length of 1.0 inch. You can then divide each centimeter into 1-millimeter intervals. These intervals will correspond to hundredths of an inch across the triangular slot.

Slide a pencil, bead, wire, string, or any other small object into the slot, as shown in Figure 8c. You can measure the object's diameter or width to the nearest hundredth of an inch and estimate the nearest thousandth.

Exploring on Your Own

Can you make a triangular slot that will measure objects to the nearest hundredth of a centimeter? Can you use it to estimate the nearest thousandth of a centimeter?

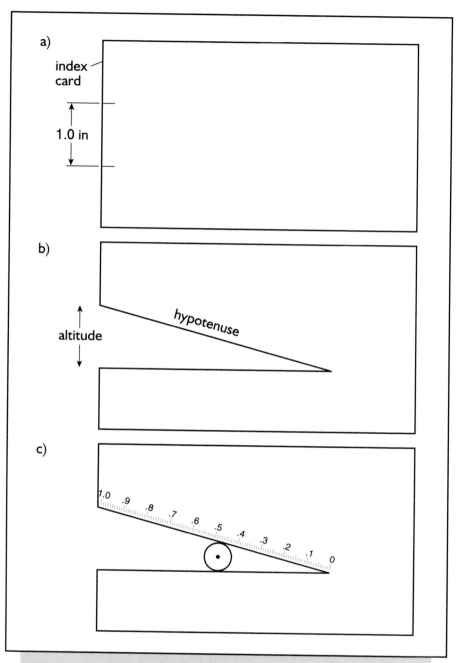

a)

index
card

1.0 in

b)

altitude

hypotenuse

c)

1.0 .9 .8 .7 .6 .5 .4 .3 .2 .1 0

Figure 8. A simple triangular slot can be used to make accurate measurements.

Invent or investigate other ways to measure small objects with great precision.

Measuring Mass

Mass, or the amount of matter in an object or a substance, is measured on a balance. Many people confuse mass and weight. An easy way to understand the difference between mass and weight is to think about taking a trip to the moon. Suppose that on the earth your mass, as determined on a large balance, is 50 kilograms (kg). Your weight—the force (gravity) with which the earth pulls you toward its center—is 490 newtons (N) as determined by a spring scale. When you reach the moon, you will find that your mass is still 50 kg. There is still the same amount of you. Your weight, however, is only 82 N because the force of gravity on the moon is about one sixth as large as it is on the earth. In other words, mass is the amount of matter in an object; weight is the force that gravity exerts on it.

A balance is used to measure mass. An unknown mass is placed on one pan (usually the one on your left). Known masses based on the standard kilogram found in Sèvres, France, are placed on the other pan until the balance beam is level. The level beam shows that the masses are equal. Because gravity pulls with the same force on equal masses, the effects of gravity cancel. Consequently, a kilogram of mass will be balanced by a standard kilogram on the moon, just as it will on the earth.

The kilogram is the SI standard measure of mass. The most common smaller unit is the gram (g), which is $\frac{1}{1,000}$ of a kilogram, but milligrams are also commonly used. You may have seen pill bottles that give the masses of chemicals in milligrams (mg). The U.S. customary system uses pounds, ounces, and a variety of other units.

You can find some of the most common units of mass and the conversions from SI to U.S. customary units and vice versa in the Appendix.

2-2*
A Balance and Standard Masses

You can make a balance from a yardstick. **Ask an adult** to drill three small holes through a yardstick, as shown in Figure 9a. The hole at the 18-inch mark should be above the center of the yardstick. The two holes one inch in from each end of the yardstick should be about ¼ inch above the lower side of the yardstick, as shown.

Push a finishing nail that fits snugly through the middle hole. The nail serves as a pivot about which the balance beam can rotate. Place the ends of that nail on two large sand-filled cans that rest on a bench or small table. Open two paper clips. Hook the wider end of each clip through the holes at the ends of the balance beam.

Things you will need:

- an adult
- drill
- yardstick
- finishing nail
- sand
- two large empty cans
- bench or small table
- two large paper clips
- string
- paper plates or small pie tins
- clay
- paper clips or small washers
- two 30-mL medicine cups
- a third calibrated medicine cup
- a number of different objects that can be weighed on the balance

Next, use string to hang paper plates or small pie tins from the paper clips at each end of the beam, as shown in Figure 9b. If the balance beam (yardstick) is not quite level, add a small piece of clay to the higher side. Move the clay closer to or farther from the center of the beam until the beam is level.

You can now use the balance to weigh a variety of small objects by seeing how much mass you must place in the right-hand pan to balance the object in the left-hand pan.

If you do not have a standard set of gram masses, you can use identical paper clips or small washers as your units of mass. To

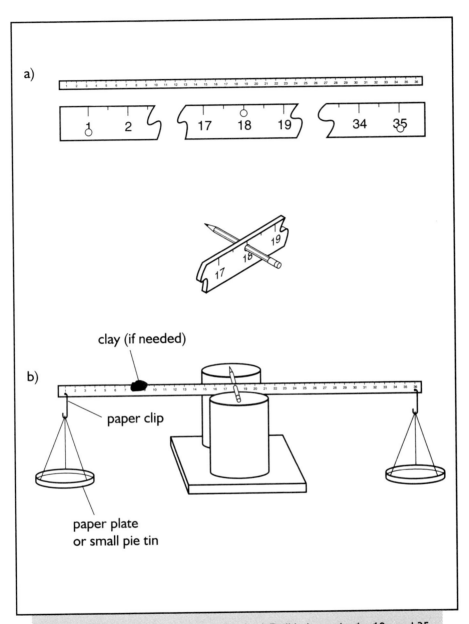

Figure 9. Make a balance from a yardstick. a) Drill holes at the 1-, 18-, and 35-inch lines. Push a finishing nail through the center hole. Use the nail to support the beam on two large cans. b) Using paper clips, string, and small paper plates or pie tins, construct and hang balance pans at each end of the beam.

convert these masses to grams, you will have to find out how many paper clips or washers equal one gram. You can do this by placing identical empty 30-mL medicine cups on opposite pans of the balance. If the beam is not level, move the clay until the beam is level. Use another calibrated medicine cup or a graduated cylinder to add exactly 20 mL of water to the medicine cup on the right-hand pan.

By definition, the mass of 1 L (1,000 mL) of water is exactly 1 kilogram or 1,000 grams (g). Consequently, the mass of 20 mL of water is 20 g. To determine the mass of a paper clip or washer, add these small masses to the right-hand pan of your balance until they balance the 20 g of water on the other pan.

Suppose the last paper clip or washer you add tips the balance beyond its level position. How can you determine what fraction of that unit of mass is needed to exactly balance the beam? Can you figure out a way to measure fractions of a gram on your balance?

Use your balance to measure a number of different objects. What is the smallest mass your balance can measure? Can you use your balance to show that air has mass? Can you use your balance to show that helium has mass? How can you change your balance so that you can measure objects with very little mass?

Exploring on Your Own

In building your balance, you were told to make the center hole at the 18-inch mark above the center of the balance beam. Why should that hole be above the center of the beam? What happens if the hole is below the center of the beam?

The world is not always what it appears to be. Our senses often deceive us. Reality and our perception of it are not necessarily the same. Sometimes measurement is the only way to prove that your senses are deceiving you.

Things you will need:

- ruler
- sand
- small jar with a screw-on lid
- large box
- balance
- people to serve as subjects for your experiments
- full moon

Lines That Deceive

Look at the drawing in Figure 10a. Does the vertical or horizontal line appear to be longer?

In Figure 10b, does the hat appear to be as wide as it is tall?

Is the upper horizontal line in Figure 10c longer, shorter, or the same length as the lower horizontal line?

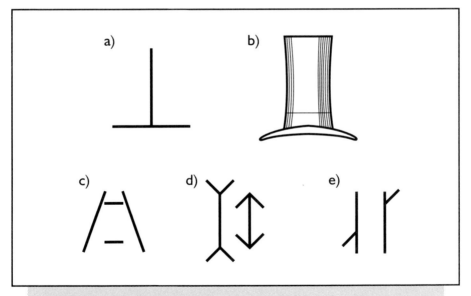

Figure 10. Lines are not always as long or as short as they appear to be.

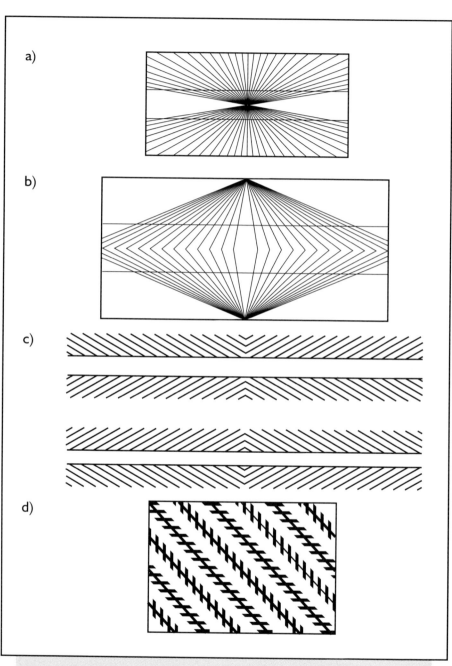

a)

b)

c)

d)

Figure 11. Parallel lines may not appear to be parallel.

Which of the two vertical lines in Figure 10d appears to be longer?

Do the two ends of the "pin through a straw" in Figure 10e actually lie along a straight line? How do they appear if you turn the book upside down? If you turn the book 90 degrees?

Are any of the horizontal lines in Figures 11a, 11b, or 11c parallel? Are the diagonal lines in Figure 11d parallel?

In Figure 12a, is the drawing inside the concentric circles a square? Is the curved drawing inside the pie-sliced circle in Figure 12b a circle? Which of the vertical posts seen in Figure 12c appears to be the tallest? The shortest?

Now go back and examine these drawings more carefully. Use a ruler to find out whether or not your answers, estimates, or decisions about length, parallelism, size, or shape are correct. What do your measurements reveal about reality as opposed to appearances?

See if you can design some illusions that appear to be different than they actually are. Develop hypotheses (possible explanations) to explain why your senses are deceived by such drawings, then try to design experiments to test your hypotheses.

Deceptive Weights

Pour some sand into a jar and screw on the lid. Then put some sand in a large box. Weigh both the jar and the box. Add or remove sand until both the box and the jar have the same weight.

Ask a friend to hold out his or her hands. Place the jar in one hand and the box in the other. Ask your friend which is heavier, the jar or the box. Repeat this experiment with a number of different people of all ages. Do they think the jar and box weigh the same? Or do they think one is heavier than the other? Develop a hypothesis to explain the results of this experiment, then try to design an experiment to test your hypothesis.

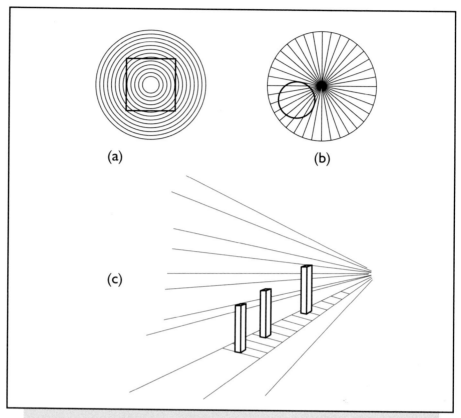

Figure 12. Shapes and sizes can be deceiving.

The Moon Illusion

Look at a full moon as it rises on the horizon. You will see that it looks a lot bigger than it does when it is higher in the sky. But how can the moon appear larger on the horizon than in the sky?

Design an experiment to actually measure the size of the moon as it appears on the horizon and then when it is higher in the sky. Is the moon really bigger when it is on the horizon?

If it is not, see whether you can develop a hypothesis to explain the reason it appears to be larger. Then design an experiment to test your hypothesis.

Measuring Areas
and Volumes

The units you read about and used in Chapter 1 to measure length, which has only one dimension, can be used to measure areas and volumes as well. Area is a measurement of surface. It has two dimensions, such as the length and width of this page. Volume is a measurement of the space occupied by something and has three dimensions, such as the length, width, and thickness of this book.

Area

The area of the surface of this page is its length times its width. This may be written as an equation:

$$\text{Area} = \text{length} \times \text{width, or } A = lw$$

To see why area is equal to length times width, think of the length, l, as a line that is "dragged" in a direction perpendicular to itself, as shown in Figure 13a. If it is dragged a distance w, it sweeps out a rectangle with a width w and a length l. Like all rectangles, it has four right angles (90-degree angles). If the length is 1 cm and the width is also 1 cm, as shown in Figure 13b, the surface will be a square. A square is a rectangle whose length and width are equal. The area within a square 1 cm on a side is said to be 1 square centimeter (1 cm^2). As you can see from Figure 13c, the number of square centimeters in any rectangle measured in centimeters is equal to its length times its width. In general, any rectangle with a length l and a width w encloses an area lw (Figure 13d). For example, a rectangle 6 cm long and 4 cm wide encloses an area of 24 cm^2 (6 cm x 4 cm). We write centimeters squared as cm^2 because, just as 2 x 2 = 2^2, so cm x cm = cm^2, inch x inch = inch^2, m x m = m^2, ft x ft = ft^2, and so on.

Significant Figures

When you multiply two numbers to find an area, your calculator may give you an answer that has more numbers than you have a right to include. For example, suppose you measure a large painting and find that it is 2.15 m long and 1.87 m wide. The fact that you write 2.15 m and 1.87 m indicates that you measured the length and width to the nearest centimeter. If you had measured to the nearest millimeter, you might have written 2.152 m and 1.870 m. The readings 2.15 m and 1.87 m each have three significant figures. The last figure in each measurement, the 5 in 2.15 and the 7 in 1.87, are estimates. In making the measurements, you decided the last figure in measuring the length was closer to 5 cm than to 4 cm or 6 cm. You also decided that the last figure in the width was closer to 7 cm than to 6 cm or 8 cm. Any numbers written after the first number you estimated would be guesses rather than estimates.

Using a better measuring device, you were able to estimate the length to the nearest millimeter. You decided the last figure in your measurement of length was closer to 2 mm than to 1 mm or 3 mm, and that the last figure in the width was closer to 0 than to 9 mm or 1 mm.

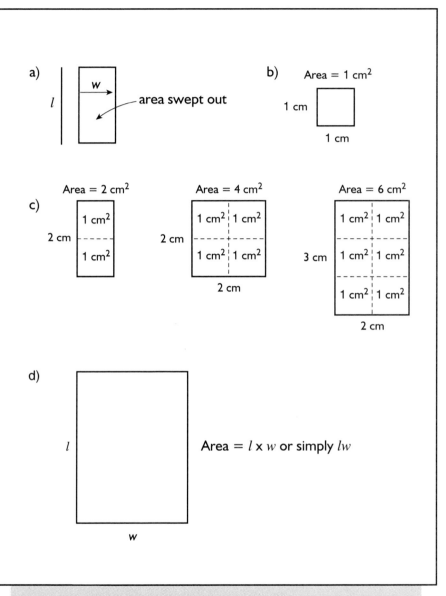

Figure 13. a) Line *l* is "dragged" in a direction perpendicular to its length through a distance *w*. b) If *l* and *w* are both 1 cm, the area swept out is 1 square centimeter (cm^2). c) As you can see, the area within a square or rectangle is equal to the length x the width. d) For any rectangle with a length *l* and a width *w*, the area it encloses is *lw*.

Let's assume the 2.15-m and 1.87-m measurements are the best you can do. To indicate that you could measure these lengths only to three significant figures, you underline the last figure in each measurement and write 2.15 m and 1.87 m. Those last underlined figures are the first ones you had to estimate in making the measurements.

To find the area of the picture, you multiply the length by the width. Your calculator tells you that the area is 4.0205. You include the units m² because you know you are multiplying meters by meters. But if you only knew each length to the nearest centimeter or hundredth of a meter, how can you know the area to the nearest ten-thousandth of a meter?

The answer is simple: You can't! The area should be expressed as 4.02 m². The area cannot have more significant figures than the least accurate measurement used to calculate it. The following equation shows why. The underlined numbers in the measurements are the ones you had to estimate, the ones of which you were unsure. In the example, any numbers that are the result of multiplication using an estimated number are also underlined. As you can see, the first digit in the answer that is uncertain, the one resulting from a column of digits containing a number based on an estimate, is in the third column. Consequently, the 2 in 4.0205 is underlined. Since it is the result of an addition involving an estimated measurement, all subsequent numbers are mere guesses. The answer should be rounded off to three significant figures, and the area should be written as 4.02 m².

$$
\begin{array}{r}
1.87 \\
\times\ 2.15 \\
\hline
935 \\
187 \\
374 \\
\hline
4.0205
\end{array}
$$

3-1*
Area and Acres

In the United States, land area is measured in acres. An acre is an area equal to 160 square rods. A rod, as you may remember from Chapter 1, is 16.5 ft or 5.5 yd. How many square feet are there in an acre? How many square yards are there in an acre?

If your family owns the land where you live, use a tape measure to measure the boundary lines. Record the data and use them to draw a map of your family's property. Then calculate the area of the property in square feet. How many acres of property does your family own? If your family does not own the land where you live, measure the dimensions of a football field or a soccer field. How many acres are included within the boundary lines of a football field? Of a soccer field? What is the area of a baseball diamond in square feet? How many acres is this?

In most other countries, land area is measured in ares or hectares. An are is 100 m². A hectare is 100 ares or 10,000 m². How many acres are there in a hectare? In an are?

Convert the areas you measured in acres to hectares. Then use a meterstick and the 1-dekameter measuring tape you made in Experiment 1-3 to remeasure the land and/or fields you measured before. From your measurements in SI units, calculate the areas in hectares. Do they agree with the areas you calculated by converting U.S. customary units to SI units?

Exploring on Your Own

If you were to paint your room, you would want to buy enough paint to cover all the surface you plan to paint. Labels on paint cans indicate that one quart or one gallon will cover a certain number of square feet. How would you decide how much paint to buy?

3-2
Area of a Triangle

You know that the area of a rectangle is equal to the product of its length and width. See if you can use this information to

Things you will need:

• sharp pencil

• paper

show that the area of a right triangle, a triangle with a 90° angle as shown in Figure 14a, is equal to ½ the base of the triangle times its height, or altitude.

Can you also show that this formula holds for any triangle, such as the one shown in Figure 14b? This is a more difficult task. However, if you extend the base of triangle ABC from BC to BD so that D lies directly under A, as shown in Figure 14c, you have another right triangle ABD. Now the task is to show that the area of triangle ABC, which is equal to the area of triangle ABD minus the area of triangle ACD, is equal to ½ AD x BC.

A trapezoid, (Figure 14d), is a four-sided figure with only two sides that are parallel. Show that the area enclosed by a trapezoid is ½ the sum of the two parallel sides times the altitude, or ½(b + d)h.

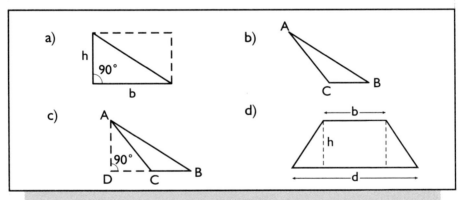

Figure 14. a) Show that the area of a right triangle is equal to ½ its base times its height (½*bh*). **b)** Does the formula ½*bh* hold for all triangles such as ABC, or only for right triangles? **c)** Can you show that the area of triangle ABC is equal to ½ (BC x AD)? **d)** Can you show that the area of a trapezoid is given by ½ the sum of the bases x the altitude, or ½(b + d)h?

3-3
Circles: Their Diameters, Circumferences, and Areas

In Experiment 1-5 you found that the ratio of a circle's circumference to its diameter was nearly constant. In fact, if you measure very carefully, you will find that ratio is a constant that is approximately 3.14. More precise measurements and mathematical theory reveal that the

Things you will need:

- drawing compass
- pencil
- sheet of thin cardboard
- ruler
- scissors
- rubber tubing

ratio is a never-ending decimal 3.14159 . . . , which is known as the Greek letter π (pi). Thus, the ratio of the circumference to the diameter is given by the equation

$$\frac{\text{circumference}}{\text{diameter}} = \pi \quad \text{or} \quad \frac{c}{d} = \pi$$

You can use this information to find a formula that will enable you to determine the area of any circle whose diameter or radius you can measure. (A circle's radius is half its diameter. It is the straight-line distance from the circle's center to its circumference.) Use a compass to draw a large circle on a sheet of thin cardboard, as shown in Figure 15a. With a pencil, mark the circle's center, which is where you placed the fixed point of the compass. Then use a pencil and ruler to draw a large number of closely spaced diameters across the circle (Figure 15b). With scissors, cut out the many narrow triangles into which you have divided the circle. The bases of all these many triangles are equal in length to the circumference of the circle, which is πd or $2\pi r$. (Of course, the bases of these "triangles" are slightly curved, but if you divided the circle into the tiniest possible sections, the bases would become straight.)

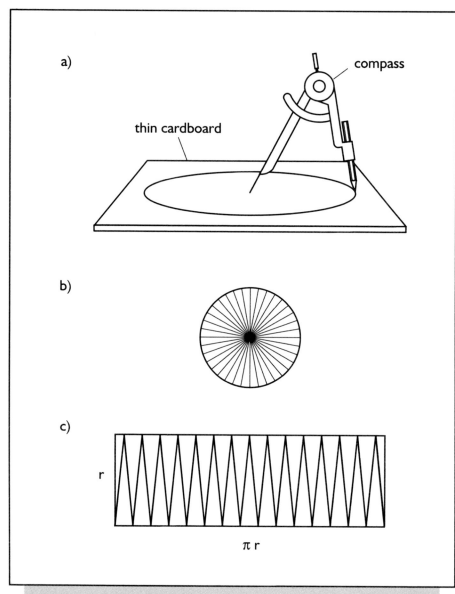

Figure 15. a) Draw a circle on a sheet of thin cardboard. b) Divide the circle into many small triangles, each with an altitude equal to the radius of the circle, r. c) Cut out the triangles and arrange them in alternate fashion to form a rectangle. The rectangle will have a width equal to the radius of the circle, r, and a length equal to half the circle's circumference, πr.

Arrange the triangles you have cut out as shown in Figure 15c to form a "rectangle." The width of this rectangle, as you can see, is the radius of the circle, *r*. Because half the triangles have their bases along the lower long side of the rectangle, the length of the rectangle is half the circumference, which is ½ π*d* or π*r*.

Since the area of the circle has been transformed into a rectangle, you can find the area of the circle by finding the area of the rectangle whose dimensions are π*r* and *r*. What do you have to know about a circle to find its area?

Another way to find the area of a circle is to break it into a series of concentric rings, as shown in Figure 16a. These rings, which can be made from rubber tubing, can be straightened out and laid side by side to form a triangle (Figure 16b). How can you find the area of a circle, using this method? Does it agree with the formula for

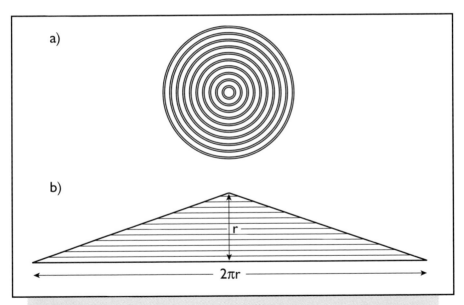

Figure 16. a) A circle is broken into a series of concentric rings. Each ring can be represented by a length of rubber tubing. b) When the rings (tubes) are straightened out and placed side by side, they form a triangle with an altitude equal to the radius of the circle, *r*, and a base equal to the circumference of the circle, 2π*r*.

the area of a circle that you found when you cut the circle into a large number of triangles?

Volume

Just as you dragged a line to sweep out an area, so you can drag an area to sweep out a volume (space). This is shown in Figures 17a and 17b. An area of 1 cm^2, if moved 1 cm in a direction perpendicular to that surface, will sweep out a cube 1 cm on a side, as shown in Figure 17b. A cube has a length, width, and height that are all equal.

The volume (space) of a cube that is 1 cm in length, width, and height is 1 cubic centimeter (1 cm^3). Again, it makes sense to label such a volume with the unit cm^3, because just as 2 x 2 x 2 = 2^3, so cm x cm x cm = cm^3. If the dimensions of an object are 2 cm x 2 cm x 2 cm, its volume is 8 cm^3 (Figure 17c). Show that the total surface area of such a block is 24 cm^2.

As shown in Figure 17d, the volume of any regular solid is given by the formula

Volume = area of base x height, or $V = lwh$.

If you rotate a rectangle or square about one of its edges, as shown in Figure 18a, you will sweep out a volume that is cylindrical. A hollow cylinder, such as a tin can, consists of two circular ends and a rectangle that has been bent to fit the circular ends (Figure 18b).

If you rotate a right triangle about one of its sides, as shown in Figure 18c, you sweep out a conical volume. What will be the shape of the volume swept out when a circle is rotated about its diameter, as shown in Figure 18d?

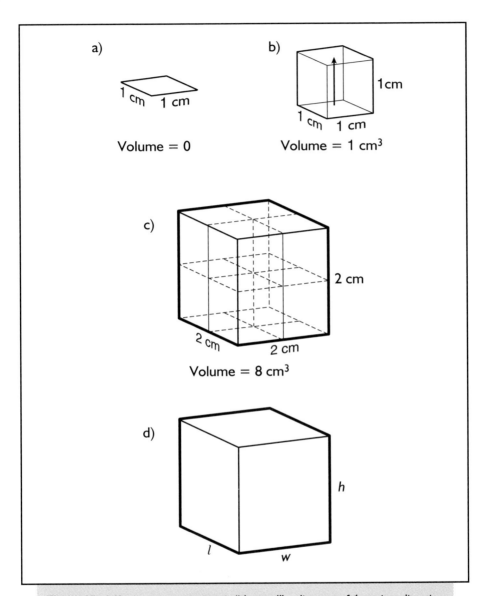

a)

1 cm 1 cm

Volume = 0

b)

1cm

1 cm 1 cm

Volume = 1 cm³

c)

2 cm

2 cm 2 cm

Volume = 8 cm³

d)

h

l w

Figure 17. a) If a square centimeter is "dragged" a distance of 1 cm in a direction perpendicular to its surface, it will sweep out a volume (space) 1 cm long, 1 cm wide, and 1 cm high. b) The volume swept out is 1 cubic centimeter (cm³). c) The volume of an object 2 cm x 2 cm x 2 cm is, as you can see, 8 cm³. d) In general, the volume of any cube or rectangular solid is equal to length x width x height (*lwh*).

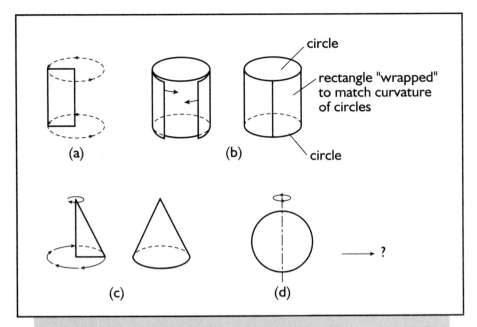

Figure 18. a) A rectangle or square rotated about one edge generates a cylinder. b) A cylinder has two circular ends. The side of it is formed by a rectangle bent to match the curvature of its circular ends. c) Rotating a right triangle about one side will generate a cone. d) What will be the shape of the volume swept out by a circle rotated about its diameter?

3-4
Working with Volumes and Surface Areas

A hands-on approach is probably the best way to understand volume. One way to get your hands into it is with some clay, from which you can

Things you will need:
- soft clay
- metric ruler

mold some cubes. With a ruler to guide you, make about a dozen clay cubes that are 1 cm on a side. Each cube will have a volume of 1 cm^3 (1 cubic centimeter).

Put four of these cubes together to make a block that is 2 cm wide, 2 cm long, and 1 cm high. As you can see, the volume of this block, which is 2 cm x 2 cm x 1 cm, is 4 cm^3. The total surface area of this block is 16 cm^2. To see that it is, simply count the number of square centimeters that you can see when you hold the block in your hand and look at it from all sides.

Take eight of the cubes you made and use them to build a cube that is 2 cm on each side. What are the dimensions of this block? What is the volume of this block, in cubic centimeters? How does the volume of this cube, which you can obtain by counting cubes, compare with the product length x width x height? What is the total surface area of this cube?

Next, use a dozen clay cubes to build a block that is 2 cm x 2 cm x 3 cm. What is the volume of this block, in cubic centimeters? How does the volume of the block compare with the product length x width x height? What is the total surface area of this block?

Now that you have seen how to build various cubes and other solids by combining cubic centimeters of clay, you can probably draw cubes and calculate their volumes and surface areas on paper. It is a lot faster than building them from individual clay cubes.

Draw cubes that are 1, 2, 3, 4, 5, and 10 centimeters on a side. Do you agree that their volumes and surface areas are those shown in Table 5?

If you do, calculate the ratio of surface area to volume for each cube. What happens to this ratio as the size of the cube increases? What significance do you think this ratio has in the natural world?

Table 5: Volumes and surface areas for different-sized cubes

Length of cube's side (cm)	Surface area of cube (cm^2)	Volume of cube (cm^3)
1	6	1
2	24	8
3	54	27
4	96	64
5	150	125
10	600	1,000

Units of Volume

By multiplying length x width x height, or area of base x height, you obtain volume, which has units equal to the unit of length cubed. For example, cm x cm x cm = cm^3, or cm^2 x cm = cm^3. Life would be simpler if all volumes were measured as cubic meters (m^3), the SI standard. However, in both the metric and U.S. customary systems of measurement, fluid volumes are commonly measured in other units. The metric system uses the liter (L), which is equal to 1 dm^3 or 1,000 cm^3 or 1,000 milliliters (mL). The U.S. customary system uses the gallon (gal), which is 231 cubic inches, as well as the quart and pint. There are 4 quarts (qt) in a gallon and 2 pints (pt) in a quart. In addition, there are fluid ounces (32 per quart), cups (4 per quart), tablespoons (½ fluid ounce), and teaspoons (⅓ tablespoon). There are also units of dry measure (pint, quart, peck, and bushel) that are different from units with the same name that are used to measure liquids.

Some common units of volume for both systems and their conversion factors are found in the Appendix of this book. For most volume measurements, we will stick with metric units.

3-5
Cylinders: Their Areas and Volumes

As you found in Experiment 3-3, the area of a circle can be found by using the formula πr^2, where r is the radius of the circle. Since a cylinder is really a rectangle bent to fit the curvature of its circular top and bottom, you can easily work out a formula to find the surface area of a cylinder.

Things you will need:

- cylindrical cardboard container
- shears
- centimeter ruler
- water
- graduated cylinder or metric measuring cup
- basting syringe or funnel

To help you arrive at such a formula, you will find it useful to take a cylindrical container apart. Remove the circular top and bottom of a cardboard cylinder such as the kind salt or oatmeal comes in. Then cut the side of the container with household shears, as shown in Figure 19.

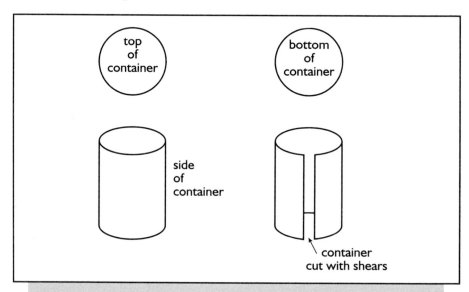

Figure 19. A cylindrical container can be dissected by removing the top and bottom, then cutting down through the side with shears.

60

To flatten the side of the container, press it against the ground with your shoe. What is the shape of the side?

The total surface area of the cylinder consists of the two circular ends and the rectangular side that wraps around to form the curved side of the cylinder. Use the parts of the cylinder you have dissected to show that the total surface area of a cylinder is equal to $2\pi r^2 + 2\pi rh$, or $\frac{1}{2}\pi d^2 + \pi dh$, where r is the radius of the cylinder (or d is its diameter) and h is its height.

The volume of a regular solid is the area of its base times its height. In the case of a cylinder, the area of the base is πr^2. If the base of a hollow cylinder has a radius of 10 cm, the area of that base is $\pi \times (10 \text{ cm})^2$, or 314 cm^2. If water is poured into the cylinder until its depth is 1 cm, the volume of water in the cylinder should be 314 cm^3. If the depth of the water is 10 cm, its volume should be 3,140 cm^3. In general, the volume should be given by the formula $\pi r^2 h$, where πr^2 is the area of the base and h is the height of the cylinder or the fluid in it.

The units are correct because a volume has three dimensions, and the units of a radius squared will be square units, such as cm^2. When multiplied by the height, h, the units become cubic. For example, cm^2 x cm = cm^3.

You can test this formula ($\pi r^2 h$) by using a centimeter ruler to measure the inside diameter and height of a can and then filling it with water. From your measurements, predict the volume of water in the can. Then pour the water into a graduated cylinder or metric measuring cup. If you have difficulty pouring the water from the can, you can use a basting syringe or a funnel to transfer the water to the graduated cylinder.

What was the volume of water in the can? (Do not be concerned if the graduated cylinder or measuring cup measures volume in milliliters [mL], because 1 mL is the same volume as 1 cm^3.) How closely does it agree with the volume you calculated using the formula?

61

3-6*
Cones: Their Surface Areas and Volumes

The surface area of a cone consists of the circular base and the slanted sides. The area of the base is simply πr^2. The area of the side can be found by dividing that surface into a large number of tiny triangles, as shown in Figure 20a. If the triangles are alternately arranged to form a rectangle, as shown in Figure 20b, the rectangle will have a height equal to the slant height of the cone, s, and a base

or length equal to ½ the circumference of the cone's base, or πr. Hence, the total surface area of the cone will be $\pi r^2 + \pi r s$.

You may also see the area of a cone expressed as
$$\pi r^2 + \pi r \sqrt{(r^2 + h^2)}.$$

This is because the slant height, s, is the hypotenuse of the right triangle *hrs* shown in Figure 20c. According to the Pythagorean theorem, the sum of the squares of the legs of any right triangle is equal to the square of the hypotenuse, also shown in Figure 20c. Since $s^2 = r^2 + h^2$, s is equal to the square root of $r^2 + h^2$

To demonstrate for yourself that the Pythagorean theorem works, draw some right triangles. Some easy ones to test are right triangles with sides that are 3 units and 4 units, 6 units and 8 units, 9 units and 12 units, and 1.5 units and 2 units. Then measure the hypotenuses and square the lengths of all three sides. You will find that the sum of the squares of the legs equals the square of the hypotenuse.

The volume of a cone can be determined by experiment. Find a hollow cylinder such as the kind that frozen orange juice comes in.

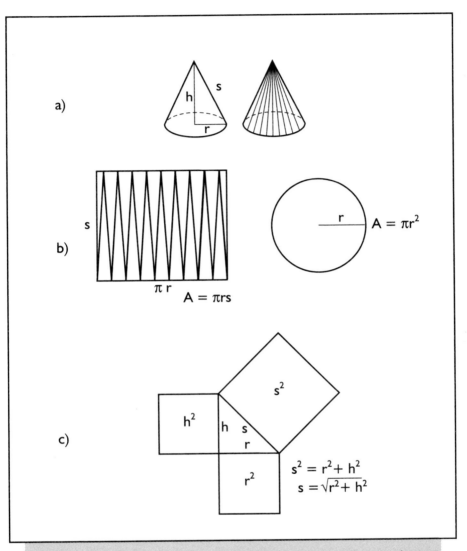

Figure 20. a) A cone's surface area can be determined by dividing its side into many tiny triangles. b) When the triangles are arranged to form a rectangle, the height of the rectangle is s, the slant height of the cone. The length of the base of the rectangle is πr, or half the circumference of the cone's base, so the area of the rectangle is πrs. The area of the cone's base is πr^2. Thus the total surface area of the cone is $\pi r^2 + \pi rs$. c) The Pythagorean theorem tells us that $s^2 = r^2 + h^2$. Therefore, the cone's slant height, s, can be obtained from the square root of $r^2 + h^2$. Consequently, the cone's area may be expressed as $\pi r^2 + \pi r \sqrt{(r^2 + h^2)}$.

Measure the inside diameter of the can. Then use a compass to draw a circle on heavy paper. The *radius* of the circle that you draw should be equal to the inside *diameter* of the cylinder. With scissors, cut out the circle and fold it along a diameter, as shown in Figure 21a. Cut the circle along that diameter. Take the half circle and form it into a cone, as shown in Figure 21b. Use tape to seal the seam along the cone's slant height.

Measure the diameter of the cone you have made. You will find it has the same diameter as the inside diameter of the cylinder. Can you explain why?

To find the height of the cone, place it next to the cylinder, as shown in Figure 21c. Use a marking pen to mark the height on the side of the cylinder, and measure that height with a ruler.

Another way to find the height is to measure the slant height. Since $s^2 = r^2 + h^2$, then $h^2 = s^2 - r^2$. Consequently, the height of the cone can be found from the square root of $s^2 - r^2$.

Mark the cone's height on the *inside* of the cylinder. Then fill the cone with salt or fine sand and pour it into the cylinder. You will find that emptying exactly 3 conefuls of the solid into the cylinder will fill it to the height you marked on the inside of the cylinder. Consequently, you know that the volume of a cone is one third that of a cylinder of the same diameter and height. Since the volume of a cylinder is given by the formula $\pi r^2 h$, the volume of a cone is $\frac{1}{3}\pi r^2 h$.

Exploring on Your Own

Show that the cone you made in this experiment has the same circumference and diameter as the cylinder you used in the experiment.

The Surface Areas and Volumes of Spheres

The surface area of a sphere is more difficult to derive. Since it is round, you can be sure π is involved, and because it is an area, r^2 will be part of the formula. One approach is to wrap string around

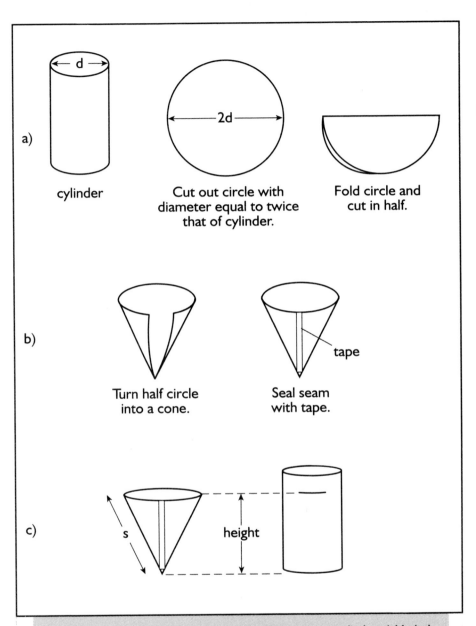

a) cylinder

Cut out circle with diameter equal to twice that of cylinder.

Fold circle and cut in half.

b) Turn half circle into a cone.

Seal seam with tape.

tape

c) s

height

Figure 21. a, b) Make a cone with the same diameter as a cylinder. c) Mark the cone's height on the cylinder. The cone's height can also be found from the slant height of the cone, s. Since $s^2 = r^2 + h^2$, $h^2 = s^2 - r^2$, and so $h = \sqrt{(s^2 - r^2)}$. Use your calculator to find $\sqrt{(s^2 - r^2)}$.

the Northern Hemisphere of a globe, as shown in Figure 22a. From the number of windings and the length and width of the string, you can find the area of half the globe. If done carefully, you will find that the area of the string is equal to π times twice the globe's radius squared. This means that the total surface area of the globe is $4\pi r^2$.

The volume of a sphere can be determined in a way that is similar to the way you found the volume of a cone. A hollow cone with a radius *and* height equal to the radius of a hollow sphere is filled with water. The cone can be filled and emptied into the sphere exactly four times (Figure 22b). At that point, the sphere will be completely filled. This tells you that the volume of a sphere is $4 \times \frac{1}{3}\pi r^3$, or $\frac{4}{3}\pi r^3$.

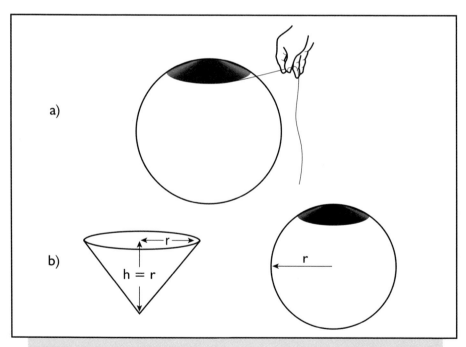

Figure 22. a) By carefully winding string around a globe, you can find the area of a sphere. b) A cone with $h = r$ and a sphere with the same radius as the cone are shown here. Four conefuls are required to just fill the sphere. Since the cone's volume is given by $\frac{1}{3}\pi r^2 h$, or, since $h = r$, by $\frac{1}{3}\pi r^3$, the sphere's volume is equal to $4 \times \frac{1}{3}\pi r^3$, or $\frac{4}{3}\pi r^3$.

3-7*
The Effect of Surface Area on the Time to Melt Ice

Will the surface area of a piece of ice affect the time it will take for it to melt? To find out, you can prepare pieces of ice made from the same amount of water that have different surface areas. You might use cube-shaped containers or large cylindrical vials to make ice pieces with a relatively small surface area. Plastic covers, such as the kind found on coffee cans or tubs of margarine, could be used as containers to make pancake-shaped pieces of ice with larger surface areas.

Things you will need:

- water
- cube-shaped containers or large cylindrical vials
- plastic covers, such as the kind found on coffee cans or tubs of margarine
- graduated cylinder or measuring cup
- freezer
- pail
- ruler
- large spoon or stick
- clock or watch with second hand or mode
- calculator (optional)

Use a graduated cylinder or a measuring cup to measure equal volumes of water. Pour the equal volumes of water into the different containers and leave them in a freezer overnight.

When you are ready to carry out the rest of the experiment, fill a pail with water. Remove two pieces of ice with different surface areas from the freezer. Quickly measure their dimensions—you can calculate their surface areas later. Place both pieces of ice in the pail of water and stir the water at a constant rate with a large spoon or stick. Which piece of ice melts first? Does surface area affect the rate at which ice melts? If it does, can you explain why it does?

Was the rate at which the ice melted proportional to the surface area of the ice?

The melting rate of ice can be measured in the units of volume of ice melted per time; that is, by volume divided by time. Such units are called derived units because they consist of more than one of the fundamental units (such as length, mass, temperature, and time).

To measure the average rate of melting, you need to know the time it took for each piece of ice to melt. Dividing the volume of ice melted by the time required to melt it will give you the average rate of melting. Of course, water expands as it freezes, so that ice occupies 1.1 times as much volume as the same mass of water. Should you take that into account as you make your calculations? If so, how?

Once you have calculated the melting rates, you can compare the ratio of the melting rates with the ratio of the surface areas to see if they are equal. If the average melting rate is proportional to the surface area, then

$$\frac{\text{melting rate of ice \#1}}{\text{melting rate of ice \#2}} = \frac{\text{surface area of ice \#1}}{\text{surface area of ice \#2}}$$

Is the average melting rate proportional to the surface area of the ice that melted? If not, can you explain why? (Another look at this experiment can be found in Chapter 4, where balances are used to measure the mass of the ice.)

Exploring on Your Own

Investigate a variety of phenomena that are affected by surface area. How does surface area affect each of them?

3-8
Shape, Surface Area, and the Time to Melt Ice

In the previous experiment, you found that the melting rate of ice is affected by surface area. In earlier experiments you found formulas that allow you to determine the volumes and surface areas of different shapes such as cubes and other rectangular-shaped solids, cylinders, cones, and spheres. In this experiment you can put your knowledge to work by making different ice shapes and predicting the order in which they will melt.

Since the time to melt is related to surface area, you might guess that for the same volume of ice, the surface area will determine the melting time. Given two pieces of ice with the same volume, you would expect the piece with the larger surface area to melt faster.

You can make pieces of ice with different shapes quite easily, as shown in Figure 23. True ice cubes can be made in cubical plastic containers or clay molds lined with plastic wrap. Cone-shaped pieces of ice can be prepared in conical paper or plastic cups. In the previous experiment, you learned how to make cylindrical pieces of ice with

Things you will need:

- cube-shaped plastic containers or clay molds
- plastic wrap
- conical paper or plastic cups
- large cylindrical vials
- plastic covers, such as the kind found on coffee cans or tubs of margarine
- balloons
- twist-ties
- clay
- plastic ice "cube" containers, small baking pans, or clay molds lined with plastic wrap
- graduated cylinder or metric measuring cup
- water
- freezer
- metric rulers
- calipers or rulers and strong rubber band
- pencil
- calculator (optional)
- paper
- sponges
- sink

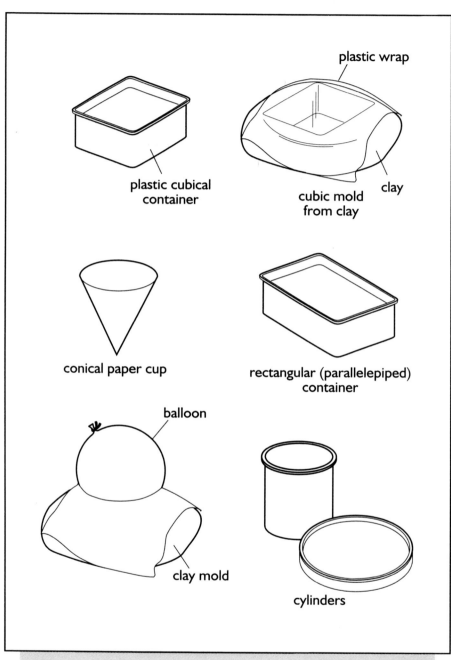

Figure 23. Ice with different shapes can be made, using a variety of containers.

small or large surface areas. Ice spheres can be made by adding water to round balloons set in rounded clay molds. The balloons can be sealed with twist-ties. Ice with three-dimensional rectangular shapes (parallelepipeds) can be made in plastic ice "cube" containers, small baking pans, or clay molds lined with plastic wrap.

Once you have prepared the molds in which to make different shaped pieces of ice, use a graduated cylinder or metric measuring cup to add the same volume of water to each mold. Why should the volume of water be the same for each piece of ice you plan to make? Why is it a good idea to make the volume of ice as large as possible?

Place the molds in a freezer overnight to be sure the water is completely frozen before you begin your experiment.

You can do most measuring of the pieces with a metric ruler, but you may find calipers useful for measuring diameters of round shapes. If you do not have calipers, you can make a reasonable

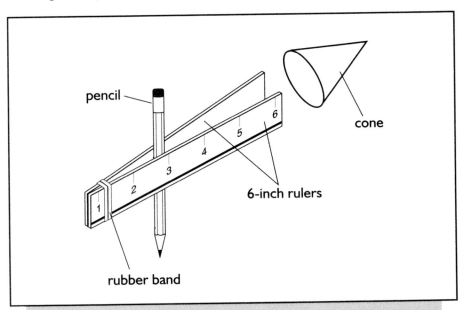

Figure 24. A pair of 15-cm (6-inch) rulers, a strong rubber band, and a pencil can serve as a substitute for calipers.

substitute. Fasten the ends of two rulers together with a strong rubber band, as shown in Figure 24. Then place a pencil between them and slide it until the ends of the rulers match the diameter you are measuring. You can place the ends of your "calipers" on another ruler to determine the measurement you have made. You will need to make careful measurements to determine the surface area of the different pieces of ice. However, you will have to measure rather quickly so that the ice does not melt. The best approach is to remove one piece of ice, measure and record your results, and then place the ice back in the freezer before you measure another piece.

After you measure the last piece of ice, allow a few minutes for all the pieces to reach freezer temperature. During that time, use your measurements to calculate the surface area of each piece. Then predict the order, from fastest to slowest, in which you think the different pieces of ice will melt.

After making and recording your predictions, quickly place each piece of ice on a sponge near the sink and wait for them to melt. Which piece melts first? Was it the one you predicted? Which is the last piece of ice to melt? Was it the piece you predicted would melt slowest?

How are the results of this experiment related to the surface area-to-volume ratios you calculated in Experiment 3-4?

4

Measuring Temperatures and Heat, Times and Speed

Temperature, as you know, is measured with thermometers. These instruments depend on fluids (liquids or gases) that expand and contract. As the environment around the thermometer becomes warmer, the fluid expands; as the environment cools, the fluid contracts.

Units of Temperature

There are several common but different thermometer scales. One was developed by Swedish astronomer Anders Celsius (1701–1744), another by German-Dutch physicist Gabriel Fahrenheit (1686–1736), and a third by Scottish physicist William Thomson (1824–1907), who was also known as Lord Kelvin.

Celsius Temperatures

Celsius calibrated his thermometer by placing it in melting ice, where the temperature was constant. He knew this because when he placed his thermometer in melting ice, the volume of the liquid mercury in the thermometer contracted to a certain level and then remained fixed. He labeled the level of mercury on his thermometer 0° as it sat in melting ice. The same thermometer was then placed in boiling water. The mercury expanded to a certain level and again remained unchanged. This showed that the temperature of boiling water is also constant. He labeled this higher mercury level in his thermometer 100°. He then divided the level between 0° and 100° into 100 equal intervals, corresponding to the 100 degrees between the freezing temperature of water (0°) and its boiling point (100°). A summary of Celsius's procedure is shown in Figure 25.

Temperatures on the Celsius scale are followed by the capital letter C, for "Celsius." Normal human body temperature on this scale is 37°C.

Fahrenheit Temperatures

In an effort to avoid negative temperatures, Fahrenheit labeled as 0° the coldest temperature he could obtain by adding salt to ice. The freezing temperature of a salt-ice mixture is well below the freezing point of water. He used human body temperature rather than boiling water as his higher fixed temperature. He then divided those two fixed temperatures into 96 degrees. Later he adjusted his scale slightly so that water froze or ice melted at 32°F and water boiled at 212°F. This made the boiling point of water exactly 180° above its freezing point. It also changed the indication of normal human body temperature to 98.6°F.

Temperatures, in degrees, on the Fahrenheit scale are followed by the capital letter F, for "Fahrenheit." Figure 26 shows Fahrenheit and Celsius thermometers side by side.

Kelvin Temperatures

Lord Kelvin (William Thomson) devised what is known as the absolute temperature scale. It is now called the Kelvin scale.

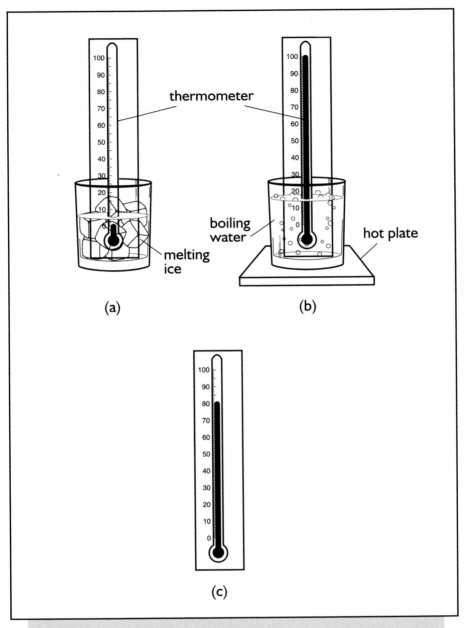

Figure 25. Celsius calibrated his thermometer by using the melting point of ice to establish a 0° mark (a), then the boiling point of water to set the 100° mark (b). c) The interval between 0° and 100° was divided into 100 equal intervals.

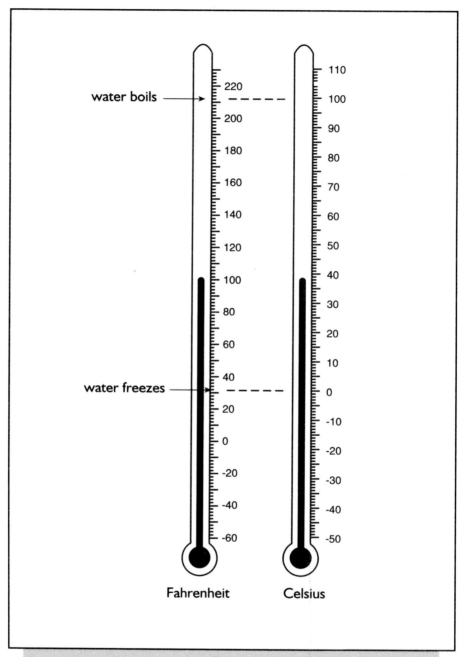

Figure 26. The Celsius and Fahrenheit scales are shown side by side.

Thomson theorized that at $-273°C$, all molecular motion would cease. Since temperature is a measure of the average motion (kinetic) energy of molecules, zero molecular speed would be the minimum possible temperature. (Kinetic energy depends on speed. If molecules have a speed of zero, their kinetic energy is also zero.)

Thomson labeled this minimum temperature absolute zero. Today we call it 0 Kelvin (0 K). Kelvin temperatures are usually expressed without a degree sign. Since Kelvin's zero point was based on a Celsius temperature ($-273°C$), he simply started his scale at $-273°C$ but called it 0. He kept the same scale difference per degree as did Celsius. Consequently, a temperature change of $1°C$ is the same as a temperature change of 1 K. Therefore, the freezing point of water on the Kelvin scale is 273 K; the boiling point of water is 100 K higher at 373 K.

Temperature Conversions

It is easy to convert from Celsius to Kelvin temperatures or vice versa because Kelvin temperatures are simply 273 degrees higher than Celsius temperatures. Consequently, $K = °C + 273$, and $°C = K - 273°$.

Formulas for converting Celsius temperatures to Fahrenheit temperatures or vice versa can be understood by studying the graph shown in Figure 27. We know that $0°C = 32°F$, and $100°C = 212°F$. These two points are used to establish the straight-line graphical relationship between these two scales.

The slope of a graph, like the slope of a hill, is the change in value along the vertical axis divided by the change along the horizontal axis. For this graph, the slope is $180°F/100°C$, or $1.8°F/°C$. But at $0°C$ the Fahrenheit temperature is $32°F$. Consequently, to convert $°C$ to $°F$, we have to add $32°$ after we multiply the Celsius temperature by 1.8. The formula for converting Celsius temperatures to Fahrenheit temperatures is, therefore, $T_{°F} = 1.8 °F/°C \times T_{°C} + 32°F$. $T_{°F}$ is the Fahrenheit temperature and $T_{°C}$ is the Celsius temperature. To convert Fahrenheit temperatures to Celsius temperatures, we must subtract 32°F and then divide by 1.8. Therefore,

$$T(°C) = \frac{T(°F) - 32°F}{1.8 \ °F/°C}$$

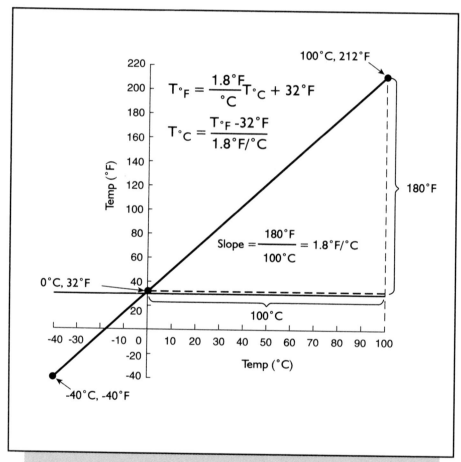

Figure 27. A graph of Fahrenheit versus Celsius temperatures shows that $T_{°F} = 1.8°F/°C \times T_{°C} + 32°F$. ($T_{°F}$ = Fahrenheit temperature; $T_{°C}$ = Celsius temperature; 1.8 °F/°C = slope of the graph; that is, $T_{°F}/T_{°C} = 1.8°F/°C$.)

4-1*
Your Temperature

Most medical thermometers in the United States are calibrated in degrees Fahrenheit. Your family probably has an oral thermometer that you can use to measure your own temperature. Digital thermometers are easy to use and to read. If you are using a mercury oral thermometer, you may want to ask an adult to help you the first time you take a person's temperature.

Things you will need:
- oral medical thermometer — digital or mercury
- alcohol
- an adult
- clock
- pencil or pen and notebook
- graph paper
- colored pencils
- a variety of people

In addition to knowing how to use and read thermometers, you will have to learn how to sterilize the thermometer with alcohol after using it.

Once you are familiar with the use of a medical thermometer, you can begin your experiment. Use the thermometer to take your temperature frequently during each day over the course of a week. Record each reading and the time in a notebook. Be sure to take your temperature when you go to bed and when you wake up, as well as during the day.

Is your body temperature constant or does it change during the day? If it changes, when does it seem to be lowest? To be highest?

Plot a graph of your temperature versus time of day on a graph like the one shown in Figure 28. Record each day's readings on the same graph. Different colored pencils can be used to connect the points for different days. What can you conclude from the graph?

If possible, ask other people to record their temperatures as you have. Do their daily temperature patterns match yours? If not, how do they differ?

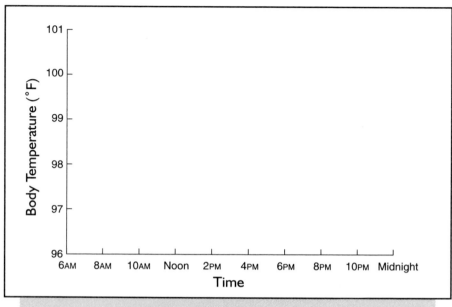

Figure 28. Use a graph with axes showing time versus body temperature to find your daily temperature pattern.

Exploring on Your Own

What is the Rankine temperature scale? How would you convert Fahrenheit temperatures to Rankine temperatures?

What is body temperature on the Rankine scale?

Where is the Rankine scale used?

Units of Heat

Heat is not the same as temperature. Temperature is a measure of the average kinetic energy (motion) of molecules. Heat is the energy transferred from a warm object to a cooler one. Unlike temperature, heat depends on mass. One gram of melting ice has the same temperature as 1 kilogram of melting ice. However, it takes 1,000 times as much heat to bring a kilogram of ice to the boiling point as it does to bring one gram of ice to boiling.

Heat can be measured in units called calories. A calorie (cal) is the amount of heat that must be transferred to one gram of water to raise its temperature by one degree Celsius. A calorie, therefore, is a derived unit. It is the product of two fundamental quantities—mass and temperature. One calorie is equal to 1 g x 1°C (1 g-°C). Consequently, if the temperature of 1,000 g of water increases from 10°C to 30°C, the heat transferred to that water is

$$1{,}000 \text{ g} \times (30 - 10)°C = 20{,}000 \text{ g-}°C = 20{,}000 \text{ cal}$$

4-2*
The Heat to Melt Ice

The temperature of water when it is melting or freezing is 0°C (32°F). This temperature, the melting or freezing point of water, does not depend on the amount of water, ice, or snow. You can prove this to yourself by placing some snow that is starting to melt in a large Styrofoam container. If you do not have any snow, you can use chopped ice. Ordinary ice cubes do not work very well because warm air can get between the cubes. Place a thermometer in the snow or chopped ice and stir until the temperature stops changing. You will find that the temperature is 0°C or nearly so. (Inexpensive thermometers are often not more accurate than a degree or two.) Now add more snow or ice to the insulated container. Does the temperature change? Does it change if you continue to add snow or ice?

Things you will need:
- water
- snow or chopped ice
- large Styrofoam container
- thermometer
- plastic dish with a capacity of 250 cm³ (8 oz) or more
- large pill bottle or a similar cylindrical container with a volume of about 50 mL
- strong rubber bands
- freezer
- graduated cylinder or metric measuring cup
- laboratory thermometer
- paper towel
- basting syringe
- eyedropper

If you are now convinced that the temperature of melting ice is 0°C, you can carry out an experiment to find out how much heat is needed to melt one gram of ice. To do this, you first need to make a block of ice with a hole in it. To make such a piece of ice, pour water into a plastic dish that holds at least 250 cm³ (8 oz) of water. A large pill bottle or a similar cylindrical container with a volume of about 50 mL should be placed in the center of the water. It can be held in place with a pair of strong rubber bands, as shown in Figure 29.

Water should surround all but the top of the empty smaller container. The water beneath it should be at least several centimeters deep. Place the container of water in a freezer overnight.

The next day, remove the container of ice from the freezer. Wait about 5 minutes for the ice to reach its melting temperature of 0°C. Then remove the rubber bands and the smaller empty container, which will leave a cylindrical hole in the large block of ice.

Use a graduated cylinder or metric measuring cup to measure out about 40 cm^3 (mL) of warm tap water. Stir the water with a

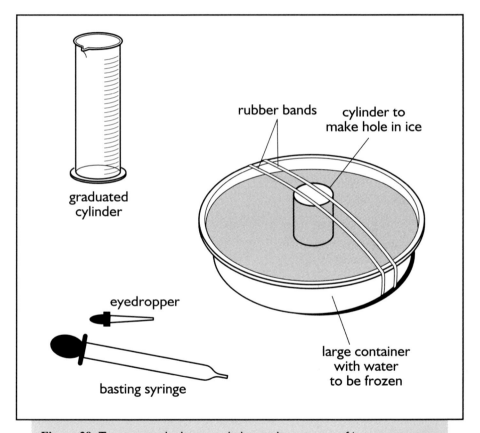

Figure 29. To measure the heat needed to melt one gram of ice, you can pour warm water into a hole in a block of ice. The drawing shows how to prepare the container before freezing.

laboratory thermometer and record the water's initial temperature. Use a paper towel to dry the hole in the ice. Then carefully pour all the warm water into the hole. Heat will flow from the warm water into the ice, causing some of it to melt and collect in the hole. The water will cool as heat flows from it to the ice. Stir the water in the hole gently with the thermometer until its temperature reaches the temperature of the ice (0°C). At that point, quickly remove all the water from the hole with a basting syringe and empty it into a graduated cylinder or metric measuring cup. You may need an eyedropper to remove the last few drops. What is the volume of the water and melted ice? How much ice melted?

The heat to melt this ice came from the warm water as it cooled from its initial temperature down to 0°C. As an example, let's assume you poured 40 mL of water at 35°C into the hole in the ice. In cooling from 35° to 0°C, it lost 40 g x 35°C = 1,400 cal to melt the ice. (Remember, a calorie is the amount of heat transferred to one gram of water to raise its temperature one degree Celsius.) If you find that the water you remove from the hole has a volume of 58 cm^3 (a mass of 58 g, since 1 cm^3 of water weighs 1 g), then 18 g of ice was melted by the heat from the warm water. Dividing the 1,400 calories of heat by the 18 grams of ice that melted gives about 78 cal/g. (Very accurate measurements give a value of 80 cal/g.) The heat needed to melt one gram of ice is called the heat of fusion for ice. According to your results, what is the heat of fusion for ice?

Exploring on Your Own

Design another experiment that will give a more accurate value for the heat of fusion for ice.

Design an experiment that will measure the heat of solidification for water; that is, the amount of heat that must be *removed* from a gram of *water* at the freezing point (0°C) to change it to a solid (ice). Do you expect this value to be different from the heat of fusion?

4-3*
Another Look at Surface Areas and Melting Rates

In Experiments 3-7 and 3-8, you found that surface area affects the melting rate of ice. However, the rate was probably not proportional to the surface area, even though that seemed a reasonable assumption to make. You may not have realized that as the ice melts, its surface area becomes smaller, so less heat can enter per unit of time. In this experiment, you will reduce the time that you leave the ice in the water so that the change in the ice's surface area will be minimal.

Make two pieces of ice that have the same volume but different surface areas, as you did in Experiment 3-7. Try to use at least 100 cm^3 of water so that your measurements will be accurate.

Things you will need:

- water
- cube-shaped containers or large cylindrical vials
- large plastic covers, such as the kind found on coffee cans or tubs of margarine
- graduated cylinder or measuring cup
- freezer
- pail or sink
- a partner
- rulers
- paper and pencil
- balance or scale to weigh ice
- two pairs of tongs
- clock or watch with second hand or mode
- paper towels
- calculator (optional)

Once the water has been in the freezer overnight and is thoroughly frozen, fill a pail or sink with water. It is good to use a lot of water, because you do not want the temperature of the water in which the ice melts to change significantly. The temperature difference between ice and water can affect the melting rate. Have a partner remove, measure, and record the dimensions of one piece of ice, while you do the same with the second.

If any significant melting occurs during the measuring process, return the ice to the freezer until it is again thoroughly frozen. Next, you and your partner can quickly weigh both pieces of ice in their containers. (You can weigh each container later and subtract its mass from the total mass to obtain the mass of the ice. Both pieces should have very nearly the same mass.)

Using tongs, you and your partner can simultaneously place both pieces of ice in the pail of water and move them about so that the ice is in contact with the water and not its own meltwater. After 10 seconds, remove both pieces of ice, quickly dry them, place them back in their containers, and reweigh them.

How much ice melted from each piece? From Experiment 4-2, you know that it takes 80 calories to melt one gram of ice. Knowing the heat needed to melt one gram of ice and the mass of ice that melted, calculate the heat that flowed into each piece of ice. Using the dimensions you measured, calculate the original surface area of each piece of ice.

Now you can find out whether or not the rate that heat flows into ice is proportional to the surface area of the ice. You can do this by comparing two ratios:

$$\frac{\text{The heat that flowed into the first piece of ice in 10 seconds}}{\text{The heat that flowed into the second piece of ice in 10 seconds}}$$

and

$$\frac{\text{The surface area of the first piece of ice}}{\text{The surface area of the second piece of ice}}$$

Do these two ratios have nearly the same value? If they do, what does this tell you? If they do not, what does that tell you?

Exploring on Your Own

How do you think the rate at which heat flows from your house or apartment is related to the surface area that is exposed to the outside air? Design an experiment to find out if you are right.

How do you think the rate at which heat flows from your house or apartment is related to the temperature difference between inside and outside air? Design an experiment to find out.

4-4*
Food and Calories

We obtain the energy we need to live and be active from the food we eat. There are three components of food from which we obtain our energy: carbohydrates, fats, and proteins. Nutritionists measure the energy we obtain from food in Calories.

Things you will need:
- calorie chart for foods
- pencil and paper
- calculator
- a number of people whose activity levels vary

Notice that their unit has a capital *C*. It is 1,000 times as large as the calorie (with a small *c*) used by chemists and physicists. A Calorie (Cal) is the amount of heat needed to raise the temperature of 1 kg (1,000 g) of water by 1°C.

Each gram of carbohydrate or protein provides 4 Calories of energy; each gram of fat provides 9 Calories, more than twice as much energy per mass as carbohydrates and proteins. During digestion, enzymes convert the carbohydrates (sugars and starches), fats, and proteins in food into simpler molecules that can be absorbed into our blood and carried to the cells of our body. Not all the food we eat is converted to energy. Some of it passes through the stomach and intestines without being absorbed. Some of the protein, after being digested, is used to make new or repair old body tissue. Consequently, the Calorie charts found in many cookbooks list the Calories per serving as less than you would expect if all the mass in the food provided energy to our bodies. For example, the Calories per serving for a 100-g hamburger (almost a quarter-pounder) might be listed as 180 Calories. Even if you made the unlikely assumption that the hamburger was pure protein, with no fat, you would have calculated an energy of 400 Calories (100 g x 4 Cal/g).

By using a Calorie chart and carefully recording the amount of everything you eat and drink each day for a week, you can estimate your average daily Calorie intake. Compare that Calorie intake with your daily Calorie requirement. Use the following chart to estimate your daily Calorie requirement. The chart shows the approximate number of Calories required per hour for various levels of activity.

Activity	Calories per hour
Sleep	65
Sitting at rest	100
Light work or activity	120
Moderate work or activity	175
Heavy work or activity	350

To determine your average Calorie intake, add the total Calories in the food you eat for several days. Divide the total number of Calories by the number of days. Now add about 10 percent of this number to your daily Calorie requirement, because the process of digesting the food requires about 10 percent of the Caloric intake. How does your daily Calorie requirement compare with your average daily Calorie intake? They should be about equal if you are not gaining or losing weight.

Exploring on Your Own

If possible, determine the daily Calorie intake and requirements for other people. Try to choose a variety of people. Choose several who are very active and several who are relatively inactive or sedentary. Which of the people you tested had the largest Calorie requirement? The smallest Calorie requirement? What is the ratio of these two values? How do the their Calorie requirements compare with their average daily Calorie intakes?

4-5*
Time and Frequency

Time, like length, mass, and temperature, is a fundamental unit. It is measured in seconds or multiples of a second, such as minutes or hours, in both SI and U.S. customary units. Frequency is a measure of the number of times something happens in one

Things you will need:
- clock or watch with a second hand or second mode
- a friend, sibling, or parent
- a number of people of different ages, male and female

unit of time. The SI unit for frequency is the hertz (Hz). One cycle per second equals one hertz (1/s). Your heart rate is measured in beats per minute. Many automobiles have a tachometer, which measures the number of times the driveshaft rotates per minute or second. The frequency at which a string on a musical instrument oscillates is measured in vibrations per second. The rate at which radiation is emitted from a radioactive substance is measured in counts per second. How many other examples can you think of in which frequency is used to measure something?

You can measure your heart rate quite easily. To do so, place your two middle fingers at a point on your body where you can feel the wave of expansion and contraction that travels along arteries with each heartbeat. The wave that you can feel is called a pulse.

There is a place on the underside of your wrist just a short distance behind the point where your thumb connects with your wrist where you can feel a pulse. Figure 30 shows you the approximate place to put your fingers to feel this pulse. Where else are arteries close enough to the surface so that you can feel their expansion and contraction?

Take your own pulse. Count the number of times your heart beats in 30 seconds. Multiply that number by 2 to find your heart's frequency in beats per minute. At what frequency does your heart beat when you are at rest?

89

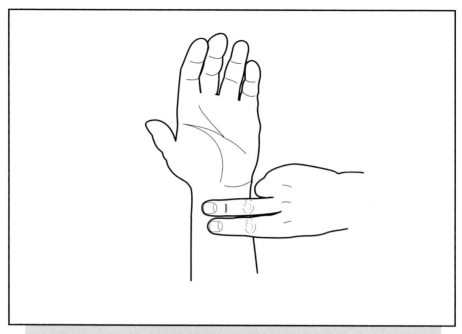

Figure 30. Use your index and middle fingers to feel for a pulse on the inside of your "patient's" wrist under his thumb.

Measure the frequency at which other people's hearts beat when they are at rest. Try to take measurements on people of all ages. Does age seem to have any effect on the frequency at which the heart beats? Do male hearts beat faster or slower than female hearts?

To see the effect of body position and exercise on frequency of heartbeat, ask a friend, sibling, or parent to lie down and relax. After a few minutes, take his or her pulse. What is that person's heart frequency while at rest?

Ask your subject to sit up for five minutes. What is his or her heart rate while sitting? Repeat the measurement after he or she has been standing for five minutes. If possible, do the same experiment on a number of different people.

Does body position have any effect on the frequency of a person's heartbeat?

Exploring on Your Own

Design your own experiment to find out how walking, running, and climbing stairs affect the frequency at which a person's heart beats. How does exercise affect the frequency of a person's heartbeat?

What do you think happens to the frequency of a person's heartbeat when he or she is asleep? Design an experiment to find out. Do some research to find out how the frequency at which the human heart beats compares with that of other animals.

4-6
Time, Frequency, and Period

For many repetitive actions, it is often more convenient to measure the period rather than the frequency. Period is the inverse of frequency. It is the frequency turned upside down. For example, Earth's period, T (the time for it to make one rotation), is one day, 24 hours, or 86,400 seconds. Its frequency of rotation is one per day (1/day), one per 24 hours (1/24 hr), or one per 86,400 s (1/86,400 s). If an engine's frequency of rotation is 1,000 per second, its period is 0.001 s or 1 s/1,000. If a repetitive motion has a frequency f, its period, T, is given by

Things you will need:

- thread
- metal nut or washer
- an adult
- sharp knife
- tongue depressor
- door frame or a chair and table
- tape
- meterstick or yardstick
- stopwatch or a clock or watch with a second hand or mode
- graph paper
- pencil
- calculator (optional)

$$T = 1/f$$

A pendulum is a device that can be used to measure time. In fact, for many years pendulum clocks were the world's most accurate time-measuring instruments. You can build a simple pendulum. To begin, tie a long piece of thread to a metal nut or washer. The nut or washer will serve as the pendulum bob. Hold the thread between the thumb and index finger of one hand so that the bob can swing back and forth, as shown in Figure 31a. The length of a pendulum is measured from its point of support to the middle of the bob. (The point of support is now your finger and thumb.) What happens to the frequency with which the bob oscillates (swings back and forth) as you make the pendulum shorter by pulling the thread upward between your thumb and finger? What

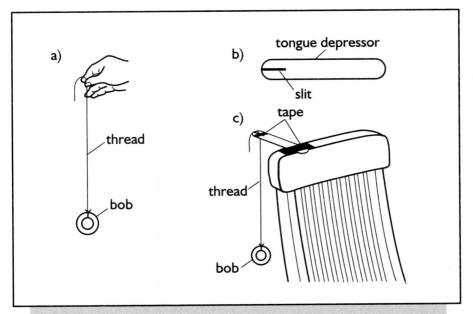

Figure 31. a) A simple pendulum can be made by hanging a nut or washer on a thread. b) Have an adult use a knife to make a slit in one end of a tongue depressor. c) Tape the tongue depressor to a door frame or chair so that the length of the pendulum can be adjusted by pulling the thread through the slit in the tongue depressor.

happens to the frequency of its oscillation as you make the pendulum longer? What happens to the pendulum's period as you make these changes?

For more careful measurements of the pendulum, **ask an adult** to use a sharp knife to make a narrow slit in one end of a tongue depressor, as shown in Figure 31b. Tape the other end of the tongue depressor to the top of a door frame or to a chair. Slide the free end of the long piece of thread into the slit in the tongue depressor. The point of support is now the bottom of the tongue depressor, so the pendulum's length is measured from the bottom of the tongue depressor to the *middle* of the bob (the nut or washer). The length of the pendulum can be adjusted by pulling the thread through the slit in the tongue depressor. To avoid changes in length while the bob is swinging, the upper end of the thread can be taped to the top of the tongue depressor (Figure 31c).

Adjust the thread until the length of the pendulum is exactly 1 m (39 ⅜ inches). Set the pendulum in motion by gently pulling the bob several centimeters to the side of its rest position and releasing it. Using a stopwatch—or a clock or watch with a second hand or mode—measure and record the time for the pendulum to make 20 complete (back and forth) swings. How can you find the pendulum's period from the data you have collected? What is its period? What is its frequency?

Why is it better to measure 20 swings rather than just one? If you do not know, try measuring the period of just one swing several times. How precisely can you measure the time for one swing? How precisely can you measure the time for 20 swings?

Next, change the length of the pendulum to 0.5 m (50 cm), or 19 ¹¹⁄₁₆ inches, and measure its period. Do you expect the period to be greater, smaller, or the same? Were you right? What is the period? What is the frequency?

Measure the period of the pendulum when its length is 0.25 m (25 cm), or 9 ²⁷⁄₃₂ inches. Measure the period of the pendulum for lengths of 0.75 m (29.5 inches), 1.5 m (59 inches), and, if possible, 2 m (78 ¾ inches).

In the experiment you just did, the variables are the length of the pendulum and its period. We say the length is the independent variable because it is the one that we change. The period is the dependent variable because it depends on the pendulum's length.

If the period of a pendulum is proportional to its length, doubling the length should double the period. Is the period proportional to the length?

If a pendulum's period is not proportional to its length, perhaps the period squared is proportional to the length. To find out if this is the case, try plotting a graph of the pendulum's period squared (T^2) versus its length (L). Use a graph like the one in Figure 32a.

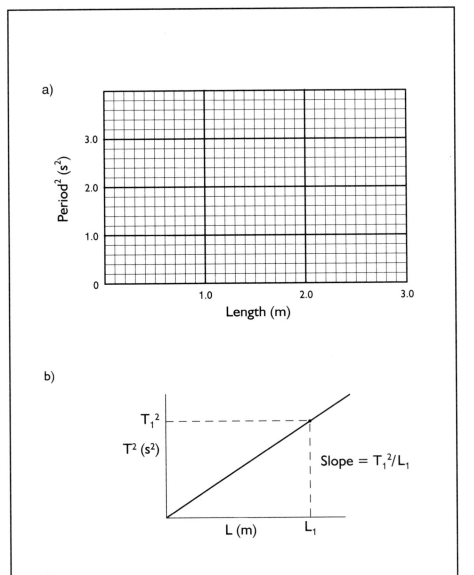

Figure 32. a) Make a graph like the one shown here and plot period squared versus length, using your data from the pendulum experiment. b) A straight-line graph of T^2 versus L would indicate that the two variables are proportional. The slope would be equal to T^2/L.

If T^2 is proportional to L, the data points should lie very close to a straight line, like the graph in Figure 32b. After making a graph based on your data, what do you conclude?

You can use your graph to write an equation such as

$$T^2 = \text{constant} \times L$$

where T is the period and L is the length. The constant is simply a number with units that relates the two variables. It is equal to the average value of T^2 *divided* by the average value of L. If the square of the pendulum's period is proportional to its length, then the slope of the graph (the rise divided by the run; that is, the change in T^2 divided by the change in L) should be equal to the constant. Since the slope of the graph would have a value of T^2 divided by a corresponding value of L, the units of the constant would be s^2/m.

4-7*
From Length and Time to Speed

By measuring length and time, you can obtain a derived unit that is used to measure speed. Speed, which is length divided by time, indicates how fast something is moving. You can measure the speeds at which some of your friends or class-mates run. Then you can compare their speeds with some of the world's fastest humans.

Things you will need:

- 10-m tape measure made in Experiment 1-3
- powdered lime or a couple of sticks
- stopwatch or a watch with a second hand or mode
- pencil and paper
- calculator (optional)

To measure a friend's average running speed, you can measure the time it takes him or her to run 50 meters. Use the 10-m tape measure you made in Experiment 1-3 to mark off a distance of 50 meters on a level field. Use a little powdered lime or a couple of sticks to mark the start and finish lines.

Have your friend get in a sprinter's start position at the starting line. You should stand at the finish line with one hand raised. Hold a stopwatch or a watch with a second hand or mode in your other hand. Your friend should start running at the moment you quickly lower your raised hand. When you see your friend start to run, start the stopwatch or note the time according to the second hand or mode. At the moment your friend crosses the finish line, stop the stopwatch or note the new time according to the second hand or mode. How many seconds did it take your friend to run the 50-m distance? Record the time on a piece of paper.

To find your friend's average running speed, divide the distance he or she ran (50 m) by the number of seconds it took to run that distance. For example, if the run was made in 8.0 s, the runner's average speed was $\frac{50 \text{ m}}{8.\underline{0} \text{ s}} = 6.\underline{3} \text{ m/s}$

(Assuming only two significant figures in the time, the speed was rounded to the nearest tenth of a second, or two significant figures. Remember, the underlined number is the first estimated unit of measure.)

Have a number of people make this 50-m run. Determine the speed of each person. Based on your calculations, predict the winner of a 50-m race among your friends.

In 1981, James Sanford ran 50.0 m at an indoor track in 5.61 s. What was his average speed for that run? What is the ratio of Sanford's speed to the speed of your fastest friend?

At the 1996 Olympics, Donovan Bailey set a world's record when he ran 100 meters in 9.84 s. What was his average speed during this run? How does his speed compare with Sanford's? How many times faster is Bailey than your fastest friend?

Based on the runs by Sanford and Bailey, it would appear that the world's best runners can run faster for 100 meters than for 50 meters. Can you explain why?

Exploring on Your Own

Under adult supervision, design and carry out an experiment to measure the speed of cars passing your school, home, or a section of highway. **Be sure to keep an eye on traffic while doing this project.** What percentage of the cars are driving at or under the speed limit? What percentage are exceeding the speed limit?

If you think cars are traveling too fast and endangering lives, you might like to share your information with the local police.

5

Indirect Measurements

You may have read that we are 150,000,000 kilometers from the sun, which has a mass, in kilograms, equal to 2 followed by 30 zeros. You may also have heard that it would take 600 sextillion protons to have a mass of 1 gram and 2,000 times as many electrons to have the same mass. Perhaps you have heard, too, that the largest animal to ever live—the blue whale—weighs as much as 200 tons, or that the earliest human ancestor to walk erect lived about 4 million years ago.

These are fascinating numbers, but no one ever weighed a blue whale, a proton or an electron, and certainly not the sun. Nor has anyone ever stretched a measuring tape from the earth to the sun. None of these measurements were made directly. They are all examples of indirect measurements, yet we accept them with as much confidence as you do when you measure your height or weight.

The Thickness of a Sheet of Paper

You would find it impossible to measure the thickness of one sheet of paper in a book, using your ruler. However, you can measure the thickness of 50 sheets (that's 100 pages because print appears on both sides of a sheet) with a ruler or one of the instruments you made in Experiment 2-1. Based on your measurement of 50 sheets, how can you find the thickness of one

Things you will need:

- this book
- ruler or the instrument you made in Experiment 2-1
- dictionary
- novel
- magazine
- paper napkins
- writing or computer paper
- string
- thread
- calculator (optional)

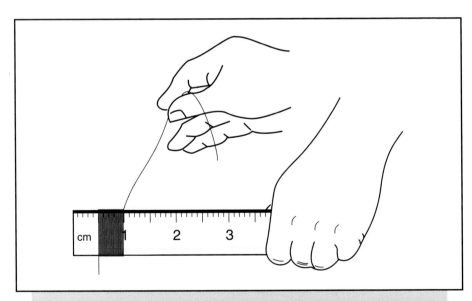

Figure 33. The width of a piece of string can be measured by wrapping the string around a ruler many times.

sheet? Would your measurement of the thickness of one sheet be more accurate if you measured 100 or 200 sheets?

How does the thickness of one sheet in the book you used above compare with the thickness of one sheet in a dictionary, a novel, or a magazine? How does it compare with the thickness of a paper napkin or a sheet of writing or computer paper?

The Thickness of a String

In theory, you could lay many pieces of string on top of one another until you had a layer that was thick enough to measure. However, such a method is not very practical. What you can do is wrap the string around a ruler so that each winding touches the previous one, as shown in Figure 33. As you wrap a large number of windings of string around the ruler, count each one until you have a width that can be measured accurately.

How can you determine the thickness of the string? How thick is the string? How thick is thread?

5-2
An Indirect Measurement of Height

Find a tall tree near your home or school or in a park. How tall is the tree? It is probably too difficult or dangerous to climb such a tree carrying a tape measure. And even if you did climb to the top, the limbs would make it difficult to establish a straight vertical distance to measure. You can, however, measure the height of the tree quite accurately, using indirect measurements. Here are two ways to do it. Perhaps you can think of other ways.

The Shadow Method

If the sun is shining, you can use similar triangles to measure the tree's height. Figure 34a shows you a pair of similar triangles. Triangles ABC and aBc share a common right angle (90°). Since their hypotenuses are parallel, angles 1 and 1' must be equal. The total number of degrees in any triangle is 180°; therefore, the third angles (2 and 2') will be equal, too. The corresponding sides of similar triangles are proportional. If you measure the corresponding sides of triangles ABC and aBc, you will see that the ratios AB/aB, BC/Bc, and AC/ac are all equal.

A tree's shadow and the length of the shadow of an upright meterstick or yardstick can be used to find the tree's height. Light rays from the sun, which are nearly parallel when they reach the

Things you will need:
- tall tree
- sunny day
- meterstick or yardstick
- sharp pencil and paper
- ruler
- two partners
- tape measure
- square sheet of cardboard about 30 cm (12 in) on a side
- protractor
- tape
- calculator (optional)
- large drinking straw
- pin
- thread
- paper clip
- steel washer, nut, or fishing sinker
- ruler

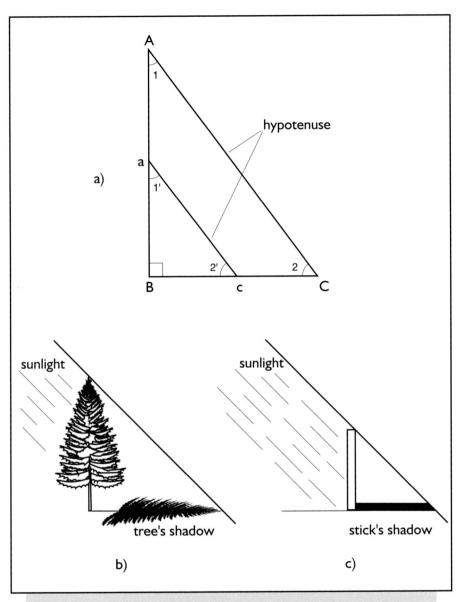

Figure 34. a) Similar triangles have equal angles, and their corresponding sides are proportional. The two right triangles ABC and aBc both have 90-degree angles at B, and angles 1 and 1′ are equal, as are angles 2 and 2′. Since the angles are equal, the triangles are similar and, therefore, AB/aB = BC/Bc, and AB/aB = AC/ac. b) A tree and a vertical stick cast shadows. The tree and its shadow form the sides of a right triangle. The sun's light rays form the hypotenuse of the triangle. A similar triangle is formed by the stick, its shadow, and more of the sun's parallel rays.

earth, form the hypotenuse of each of the similar triangles shown in Figure 34b. Since the triangles are similar, the ratio of the tree's height to the length of its shadow is the same as the ratio of the meterstick's height to the length of its shadow. Why must both shadows be measured at approximately the same time?

If the length of the meterstick's shadow is 30 centimeters (cm), the stick is 3.33 times as long as its shadow. The height of the tree, therefore, must be 3.33 times the length of its shadow. If the tree's shadow is 6 meters long, the height of the tree is 3.33 x 6 m, or 20 m.

A Ratio Method

On a cloudy day, you can use a somewhat less accurate method that is sometimes used by artists. Have a friend stand next to the tree, flagpole, or building that you want to measure, while you stand about 20–50 m (60–170 ft) away. Hold a 30-cm (12-inch) ruler upright at arm's length, as shown in Figure 35. Line up the zero end of the ruler with your friend's feet. Then move a pencil along the ruler with your other hand until it is in line with the top of your friend's head. The length equal to the distance between the end of the ruler and the pencil represents your friend's height as seen from your position. Ask a partner to record that length. Then, from the same position, use the same method to find the length along the ruler that represents the height of the tall object. What is the ratio of the tree's height to your friend's height?

Measure your friend's height as accurately as possible. You know the ratio of the tree's height to your friend's height. How can you use that ratio and the known height of your friend to find the height of the tree?

Use what you know about circles and a tape measure to find the diameter of the tree's base.

An Angular Method

Having seen how similar triangles can be found among tall objects, sunlight, and shadows, you will probably not be surprised to learn that angles can be used to make indirect measurements.

To measure angles, you will need an astrolabe like the one shown in Figure 36a. You can make an astrolabe from a square sheet

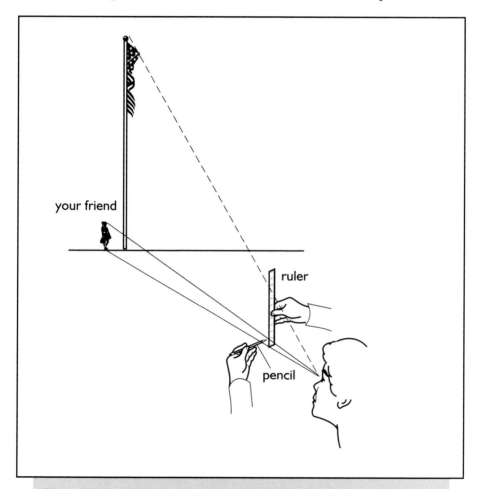

Figure 35. On a cloudy day you can find the height of a tall object by finding the ratio of the object's height to the known height of a person or other object next to it.

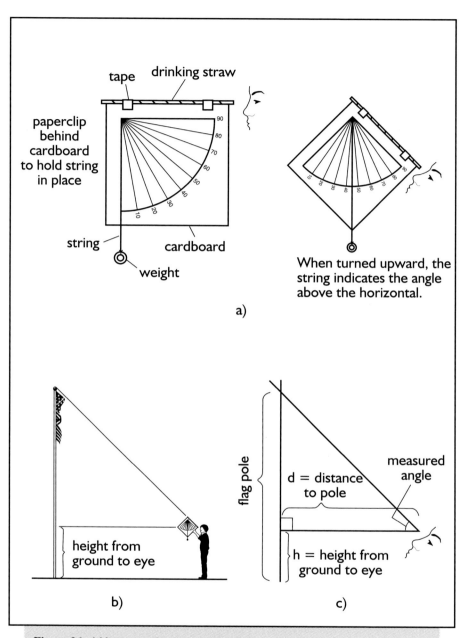

Figure 36. a) You can make an astrolabe that can be used to measure angles. b) Use your astrolabe to measure a tall object such as a flagpole. c) Make a scale drawing to find the height of the tall object.

of cardboard about 30 cm (12 in) on a side. Using a protractor, mark off angles from 0 to 90 degrees, as shown. Then tape a large-diameter drinking straw to the top of the cardboard. Use a pin to make a hole at the point where all the degree lines meet. Thread a string about 45 cm (18 in) long through the hole. Tie the end of the string to a paper clip to prevent it from slipping back through the hole. To the other end of the string, tie a steel washer, a metal nut, or a fishing sinker. The metal weight and string serve as a plumb line that will always extend down toward the center of the earth.

You can use your astrolabe to measure the height of tall objects such as flagpoles, trees, and buildings. Figure 36b shows how your astrolabe can be used to measure the height of a flagpole. Stand a known distance from the base of the pole. Use the astrolabe to measure the angle that the top of the pole makes to the horizontal at your eye level. Using the angle you have measured and the distance to the vertical flagpole, you can draw a triangle to scale, as shown in Figure 36c. For example, 1 cm on your scale could represent 1 m of distance along the ground. The triangle's base is the scaled distance from the flagpole to the point where you stood to make your measurement with the astrolabe. The triangle's hypotenuse will lie along the angle you measured. The intersection of the hypotenuse and the vertical line representing the flagpole will give you the scaled height of the pole. Simply measure that vertical line to find out how high the pole's top is above your eye. By adding the height of your eye above the ground, you can find the total height of the pole.

Use your astrolabe, a tape measure, a ruler, a pencil, paper, and a protractor to find the height of a number of tall objects.

You can also use your astrolabe to measure the angular height of the moon or stars above the horizon, or the angular separation of stars and other celestial bodies. Why can't you use your astrolabe to measure the distances to stars or planets?

5-3*
Using a Known Height to Measure Distance Indirectly

In the previous experiment you used a friend's known height to measure the height of a tree. Knowing your friend's height and the ratio of the tree's height to that of your friend, you were able to measure the tree's height indirectly.

You can use that same friend, or any object of a known height, to measure horizontal distance as well. Ask your friend to stand at some point to which you wish to know the distance. It might, for example, be the distance to the opposite side of a river. Move a small object such as a penny, bead, or button along a meterstick or yardstick, one end of which is next to your eye. When the small object appears to have the same height as your distant friend or other object of known height, record the distance of the small object from your eye. Record, also, the height of the small object.

Things you will need:

- friend or object of a known height
- small object such as a penny, bead, or button
- meterstick or yardstick
- paper and pencil
- playground, school, river or stream, familiar object seen from bedroom window, or other distant objects

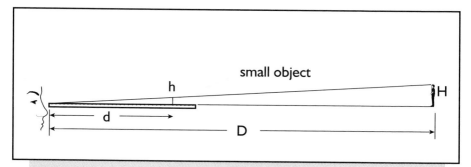

Figure 37. With a meterstick or yardstick, a small object, and a larger object of known height, you can measure large distances.

As you can see from Figure 37, the height of the small object, h, and the distance to it, d, form two sides of a right triangle that is similar to a larger right triangle. The sides of the larger triangle are the height of your friend (or other large object of known height), H, and the longer distance, D, to him or her. Because the triangles are similar, their sides are proportional. Consequently,

$$\frac{h}{d} = \frac{H}{D}$$

Since you know the ratio of h to d (h/d) and the larger height, H, of the person or object, you can calculate D. For example, if h is 1.00 cm, d is 75.0 cm, and H is 1.50 m, then D is 75 times as big as H, or 113 m.

Use this method to determine such distances as the length of your playground or school, the width of a river or stream, the distance from your bedroom window to a familiar object, the length of a block in your town or city, or some other large distance you would like to measure.

Exploring on Your Own

The moon is known to have a diameter of 3,500 km. Use this information together with your meterstick or yardstick and small object to determine the distance to the moon. Repeat your measurement of the distance to the moon at different times of the year. Is the distance between the earth and the moon always the same? How can you tell?

5-4*
Scaling: Measuring Long Distances with Maps

Maps are representations of parts of the earth's surface that have been reduced in size. The reduction is done by scaling. Large distances along the earth's surface are represented by much shorter lengths on a map. Each kilometer or mile of distance on the earth is represented by a

Things you will need:
- small washer or bead
- nail or wire such as a paper clip
- marking pen or nail file
- road map with scale
- automobile with odometer
- an adult

much smaller length on the map. Most maps have a diagram showing the scale. For example, a centimeter or an inch on the map could represent a length of 10 kilometers or 10 miles on the earth's surface. Scales commonly used by the U.S. Geological Survey are 1:25,000; 1:50,000; 1:100,000; 1:500,000; 1:1,000,000; and 1:10,000,000. A scale of 1:1,000,000 means that a length of 1 cm on the map represents 1,000,000 cm or 10 km of actual length on the earth.

Architects do the same thing in three dimensions. In preparing a scale model of a skyscraper, they might let 1 mm represent 1 m. Dollhouses are often scale models of real houses.

In Experiment 1-6 you saw how distances can be measured along the earth, using a wheel. On a smaller scale, you can use a wheel to measure distances on a road map. To do so, you will need a small wheel. You can make such a wheel from a small washer or bead mounted on a nail or wire.

Make a mark or scratch on the circumference of the wheel so that you can count the number of times it turns as you roll it along the map. You will need to know how many miles or kilometers the wheel covers along the map with each turn. This can be determined by rolling the wheel along the scale found on the map. If a turn of your wheel exceeds the scale on the map, you can extend the scale with a ruler.

Now that you know the distance in kilometers or miles on the map represented by one turn of the wheel, you can predict how many miles you will travel on the next family automobile trip. Ask a parent to show you the roads you will follow on the trip. Then roll your wheel along the roads to your destination. Count the number of turns and estimate any fractional turns of the wheel. You should then be able to predict the distance you will travel.

To check your prediction, record the car's odometer reading at the start of the trip. Record it again at the end of the trip. How does your prediction of the trip's length compare with the difference in odometer readings before and after the trip?

Exploring on Your Own

Build a three-dimensional scale model of your home or apartment. You might use your home as a model for a dollhouse you could build for a younger sibling, cousin, or friend.

5-5*
Measuring Large Distances on a Globe

A globe is a scale model of the entire earth. Somewhere on the globe you will find the scale factor that the manufacturer used in making the globe. For example, on my globe, 1 centimeter is equal to 418 kilometers, and 1 inch is equal to 660 miles. What is the scale on your globe?

Things you will need:

- globe
- string
- ruler, meterstick, or yardstick
- calculator (optional)

Use a string to measure the length from New York to Chicago on the globe. Then place that length of string next to a ruler. What length of string represents the distance from New York to Chicago? According to the globe's scale, what is the actual distance between these two cities?

Use the same string to measure the globe's circumference at its equator. What is that distance when scaled up to real lengths? How closely does the distance you calculated agree with the actual circumference of the earth, which is 40,000 km or 24,900 miles?

Use the string and a meterstick or yardstick to measure large distances on the globe, such as the distance from New York to Tokyo. You will find that the shortest distance between these two cities is along an arc that passes close to the North Pole. What is that distance?

Airplanes flying from New York to Tokyo head north rather than directly west. Do you see why? How much farther would airplanes have to fly if they followed a route west from New York to Tokyo?

Use the same method to find the shortest flight distances between some other major cities, such as Los Angeles and Bombay, Dallas and Moscow, New Orleans and Peking, San Francisco and Oslo, as well as some of the long airplane trips you may have taken or would like to take.

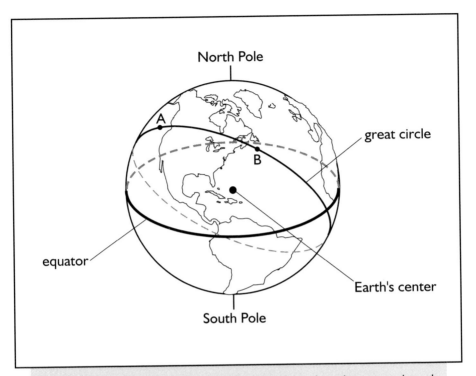

North Pole

A

great circle

B

equator

Earth's center

South Pole

Figure 38. A great circle on the globe is formed by a plane that passes through the earth's center. The shortest path between points A and B is along the great circle on which they lie.

These shortest flight routes are along what are called great circles. A great circle (Figure 38) is formed by a plane (a flat surface) that passes through the center of the earth and the earth's surface. The shortest distance between any two points on the earth's surface lies on the circumference of a great circle that includes the two points. As you have learned in this experiment, other paths are longer.

Exploring on Your Own

Do any lines of longitude lie along great circles? Do any lines of latitude lie along great circles? Why do ship captains often choose not to follow a great circle route?

Astronomical Distances

In astronomy books, you might find a table like Table 6, which lists a number of stars and their distances from the earth.

Table 6: Some well-known stars with their distances from the earth as measured in light-years

Star's Name	Distance from the earth in light-years
Alpha Centauri	4.2
Barnard's star	6.0
Sirius	8.8
Altair	17
Vega	26
Arcturus	36
Castor	45
Capella	46
Aldebaran	68
Spica	260

Notice that the distances to these stars are measured in light-years. A light-year is the distance light travels in one year. This means that the light we see when we look at the star Spica left that star 260 years ago, during Colonial times in America.

5-6
A Research Project and a Calculation Project

Do some research to find out how astronomers use parallax to measure the distance to nearby stars, such as the ones in Table 6. Then try to find out how they measure the distance to stars and galaxies that are thousands, millions, and billions of light-years from us.

Things you will need:

- library
- computer access to the Internet (optional)
- index cards
- pen
- calculator (optional)

Light travels at a speed of 300,000 km/s. Do some calculating to determine what distance, in kilometers, is equal to a light-year. What is the length of a light-year in miles? Sirius is the brightest star in the sky. In kilometers, how far from the earth is Sirius? If you were in a spaceship traveling at an average speed of 300 km/s, how long would it take you to reach Alpha Centauri, the closest star to the earth (other than our sun)?

5-7*
How Big Is a Drop?

What is the volume of a drop of water? If you put a drop of water or any other liquid into a graduated cylinder, you can hardly see it. But if you use a technique that is similar to the method you used to find the thickness of a sheet of paper, you can measure the volume of a drop.

Things you will need:
- eyedropper
- water
- graduated cylinder or metric measuring cup
- paper and pencil
- calculator (optional)
- paper towels

Take a graduated cylinder—a 10-mL graduated cylinder works well, but you can use a larger cylinder or metric measuring cup. Be sure the container is empty, clean, and thoroughly dry. Use an eyedropper to add water drop by drop to the cylinder. Count all the drops you have added until you reach the 10 mL or 100 mL line. Be sure to use the meniscus—the bottom of the curved liquid surface (shown in Figure 39)—to measure the volume of the liquid. The meniscus should be on the line that measures volume.

Use the total volume and the number of drops you have added to find the volume of a single drop. What is the volume of one drop?

Exploring on Your Own

Does the size of a drop depend on the liquid? To find out, measure the size of drops of water, rubbing alcohol, cooking oil, and soapy water. Be sure to thoroughly clean and dry the eyedropper before using it in a different liquid.

Are the drops the same size for all liquids? If not, which liquid has the largest drops? The smallest drops? How can you explain any difference in drop size between one liquid and another?

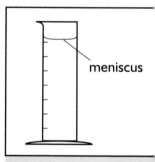

Figure 39. Because water and some other liquids adhere to glass and some plastic, the liquid surface in a cylinder is curved. Measure the liquid level at the bottom of the meniscus.

5-8
Measuring the Volumes of Irregular Objects

In Chapter 3 you learned how to measure the volume of objects or spaces with regular shapes such as cubes and other rectangular solids, cylinders, cones, and spheres. But not all objects have a regular shape. For example, a stone is unlikely to have any regular shape, but it certainly occupies space, and it will displace its own volume when placed in water or any other liquid.

To find the volume of a stone, fill a graduated cylinder or metric measuring cup to a convenient level with water. Record the water level in the cylinder or cup. Then carefully slide the stone into the water. What happens to the water level in the cylinder or cup? How can you use that new water level to find the volume of the stone?

Things you will need:

- a stone
- graduated cylinder or metric measuring cup
- water
- pencil and paper
- dry sand, both coarse and fine
- plastic or glass container about 200 mL, preferably with pour spout
- large, irregularly shaped objects
- large container through which you can see the level of the water within it
- marking pen
- thin sticks or pins
- vessel that has a spout such as a half-gallon milk carton or similar container

Suppose instead of a solid stone you want to measure the volume of some dry sand. Sand consists of tiny grains. These dry grains pile together with air spaces between them. How can you measure the volume of the sand alone?

Again, the answer is to add the sand to a known volume of water. The spaces between the grains will then be occupied by water rather than air. The space occupied by the sand grains will displace the water, causing its level to rise in a container.

117

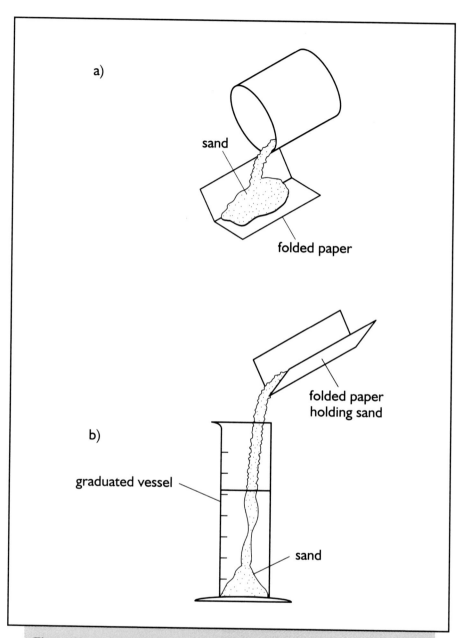

a)

sand

folded paper

b)

folded paper
holding sand

graduated vessel

sand

Figure 40. a) If you do not have a beaker or container with a pour spout, pour the sand (or part of it at a time) onto a folded piece of paper. b) Then use the paper to pour the sand into the graduated vessel.

To find out what fraction of the space occupied by dry sand is air, pour some sand into a graduated cylinder or metric measuring cup until it is about half full. Record the volume of the sand and the air it encloses. Then pour the dry sand into an empty container. Add water to the graduated cylinder or cup until it is about half full. Carefully record the volume of water in the cylinder or cup. Then slowly pour the dry sand into the known volume of water in the graduated cylinder or measuring cup. If the sand is in a container that has a pour spout, you can pour it directly from the container into the water. If it does not have a pour spout, you may want to pour it onto a folded piece of paper and then use the folded paper to add the sand to the water (see Figure 40).

What is the level of the water in the graduated cylinder or measuring cup after you have added the sand? What is the volume of the sand? What was the volume of the dry sand when it contained air? What fraction of the volume of dry sand was air? What percentage of the volume of dry sand was air?

Repeat the experiment, using a coarser or finer grade of sand. Does the percentage of air in sand depend on the size of the grains?

Measuring the Volume of Large Objects

Some irregularly shaped objects are too big to fit into a graduated vessel. The volume of such objects can be measured by placing them in a large container partially filled with water. If possible, use a container through which you can see the level of the water within it. Use a marking pen to mark the water level on the side of the container. Then place the large object whose volume you want to measure in the water. There should be enough water to cover the object completely. Mark the new water level on the side of the container. If the object floats, use thin sticks or pins to submerge it while someone else marks the new water level.

Remove the large object from the container. If it takes water with it, you will have to add water to the container to bring it to its original level. Next, pour measured volumes of water into the container until the level rises to the second line you marked on the container. How much water did you add? What was the volume of the large object?

Use this method to measure the volume of your fist. How does the volume of your fist compare with the fists of other people? Be sure all fists are submerged to the same level. You might draw a line with a felt pen at ends of the lower arm bones, which can be felt at the wrist, to mark the end of a fist.

Another way to measure the volume of large or irregular objects is to place them in a vessel that has a spout. You can make such a vessel from a half-gallon milk carton or similar container.

Fill the container with water until it comes out the spout. With the container filled with water, place a graduated cylinder or metric measuring cup under the spout. Then slowly lower the object whose volume you want to measure into the water-filled container. The object will displace its own volume of water, which will flow into the graduated vessel. What is the volume of the irregular object?

Can you use this method to measure the volume of your fist? If you can, how does this measurement compare with the previous one?

5-9*
Measuring the Volumes
and Surface Areas of People

Design a way to magnify the methods you used in the previous experiment so that you can measure the volumes of different people. **Under adult supervision,** build such a device and use it to measure the volumes of people.

Things you will need:
- an adult
- roll of wrapping paper
- scissors
- ruler or meterstick
- calculator (optional)
- a variety of people of all shapes, sizes, and ages

To measure a person's surface area, you can use wrapping paper. Cut the paper closely to fit arms, legs, neck, and body. Then unwrap it and cut it into convenient squares, rectangles, triangles, and trapezoids, which you can easily measure. From your measurements, calculate the surface areas. A similar method can be used for hands, feet, fingers, and toes. Determining the area of a person's head will require time and attention to detail. However, you might consider the top of round-headed people to be half a sphere and assume the area of that part of the head to be equal to $2\pi r^2$.

Find the surface area-to-volume ratio for each person you measure. Try to measure people of all shapes, sizes, and ages. Does a person's surface area-to-volume ratio seem to be related to age? To height? To weight?

Which of the people you measured for volume and surface area do you think would be most uncomfortable in hot weather? Why do you think so? Which of the people you measured do you think would be most likely to bundle up in many layers during cold weather? Why do you think so?

Exploring on Your Own

How is the surface area-to-volume ratio of an animal affected by its size?

How is an animal's surface area-to-volume ratio related to the environment in which it can live?

5-10*
Indirect Measurements of Mass

Masses Too Small to Weigh

On most balances you probably could not weigh a grain of rice. But perhaps you can weigh 100 grains or, if not 100, then 1,000 grains. Count out as many grains of rice as you need to get an accurate reading on a balance. Record the number of grains and their total mass. Use the information you have recorded to calculate the average mass of one grain of rice.

Things you will need:

- box of rice
- balance for weighing
- large log or large piece of lumber
- meterstick or yardstick
- calculator (optional)
- saw
- an adult
- paper and pencil
- boulder
- large tank of water

Masses Too Large to Weigh

Look for a large log or piece of lumber that is clearly too large to weigh on a balance. Measure the dimensions of the wood and calculate its volume. Then, with permission from whoever owns the log or lumber and **under adult supervision,** cut off a small sample that can be weighed on a balance.

Measure and weigh the wood sample you have collected, and record all the data. Use your measurements to calculate the volume of the sample. Then divide the mass of the wood by its volume. This will give you the density of the wood; that is, its mass per volume in grams per cubic centimeter (g/cm^3). The units of density, such as g/cm^3, are a derived unit. They are the combination of the units of two fundamental quantities, mass (g) and length (cm).

If you know the mass of one cubic centimeter, you can calculate the mass of any number of cubic centimeters. Simply multiply the density by the volume. As you can see, the product of these units gives grams (a unit of mass), which is what you want.

$$\frac{g}{cm^3} \times cm^3 = g$$

How can you use the information you have collected to find the mass of the large log or piece of lumber? How can you use this method to find the mass of a boulder? How can you use this method to find the mass of water in a large tank?

Exploring on Your Own

Atoms and molecules are much too small to weigh on even the most sensitive balance. Yet the masses of these tiny particles can be found in many chemistry and physics textbooks. Do some research to find out how such small masses can be determined by indirect methods.

Appendix

Conversions Between U.S. Customary and Metric Units

Length:

U.S. Customary Unit	Metric Measurement of the same length	Metric Unit	U.S. Customary Measurement of the same length
1 inch	2.54 cm or 25.4 mm	1 cm or 10 mm	0.3937 in
1 foot	30.48 cm or 0.3048 m	1 dm or 0.1 m	3.937 in or 0.328 ft
1 yard	91.44 cm or 0.9144 m	1 m or 100 cm	39.37 in or 3.28 ft
1 rod	502.92 cm or 5.0292 m	1 dam or 10 m	32.8 ft or 10.94 yd
1 mile	1,609 m or 1.609 km	1,000 m or 1 km	0.6215 mi or 3,281 ft

Volume:

U.S. Customary Unit	Metric Measurement of the same volume	Metric Unit	U.S. Customary Measurement of the same volume
1 cubic inch	16.39 cm^3 or 16.39 mL	1 cm^3 or 1 mL	0.061 in^3
1 cubic foot	0.0283 m^3 or 28.3 L	1 dm^3 or 1 L	61 in^3 or 1.06 qt
1 fluid ounce	29.6 mL or 0.0296 L	1 cm^3 or 1 mL	0.061 in^3
1 pint (16 fluid ounces)	473 mL or 0.473 L	—	—
1 quart	0.946 L or 946 cm^3	—	—
1 gallon or 231 in^3	3.785 L	—	—
1 cubic yard	0.7646 m^3 or 764.6 L	1 m^3 or 1,000 L	35.3 ft^3
1 cubic mile	4.17 km^3	1 km^3	0.24 mi^3

Mass:

U.S. Customary Unit	Metric Measurement of the same mass	Metric Unit	U.S. Customary Measurement of the same mass
1 grain	64.8 mg	1 mg	0.0154 grain
1 dram	1.772 g or 177.2 mg	1 g or 1,000 mg	0.564 dram
1 ounce	28.35 g or 0.02835 kg	1 g or 1,000 mg	0.0353 ounce
1 pound	453.6 g or 0.4536 kg	1 kg	2.2 pounds
1 ton or 2,000 pounds	0.907 metric tons	1 metric ton or 1,000 kg	2,200 pounds

List of Suppliers

Carolina Biological Supply Co.
2700 York Road
Burlington, NC 27215
(800) 334-5551
http://www.carolina.com

Central Scientific Co.
(CENCO)
3300 Cenco Parkway
Franklin Park, IL 60131
(800) 262-3626
http://www.cenconet.com

Connecticut Valley Biological
Supply Co., Inc.
82 Valley Road, Box 326
Southampton, MA 01073
(800) 628-7748

Delta Education
P.O. Box 915
Hudson, NH 03051-0915
(800) 258-1302

Edmund Scientific Co.
101 East Gloucester Pike
Barrington, NJ 08007
(609) 547-3488

Fisher Science Education
485 S. Frontage Road
Burr Ridge, IL 60521
(800) 955-1177
http://www.fisheredu.com/

Frey Scientific
100 Paragon Parkway
Mansfield, OH 44905
(800) 225-3739

Nasco-Fort Atkinson
P.O. Box 901
Fort Atkinson, WI 53538-0901
(800) 558-9595

Nasco-Modesto
P.O. Box 3837
Modesto, CA 95352-3837
(800) 558-9595
http://www.nasco.com

Sargent-Welch/VWR Scientific
P.O. Box 5229
Buffalo Grove, IL 60089-5229
(800) SAR-GENT
http://www.SargentWelch.com

Science Kit & Boreal
Laboratories
777 East Park Drive
Tonawanda, NY 14150
(800) 828-7777
http://sciencekit.com

Ward's Natural Science
Establishment, Inc.
P.O. Box 92912
Rochester, NY 14692-9012
(800) 962-2660
http://www.wardsci.com

Further Reading

Books

Adams, Richard, and Robert Gardner. *Ideas for Science Projects.* Revised edition. Danbury, Conn.: Franklin Watts, 1997.

Ash, Russell. *Incredible Comparisons.* Boston: Houghton Mifflin, 1996.

Cook, Nancy, and Christine V. Johnson. *Measuring Dinosaurs.* Reading, Mass.: Addison Wesley, 1995.

Gardner, Robert. *Science Projects About Math.* Springfield, N.J.: Enslow Publishers, Inc., 1999.

Gardner, Robert, and Eric Kemer. *Science Projects About Temperature and Heat.* Hillside, N.J.: Enslow Publishers, Inc., 1994.

Markle, Sandra. *Measuring Up: Experiments, Puzzles, and Games Exploring Measurement.* New York: Atheneum, 1995.

Robson, Pam. *Clocks, Scales, and Measurements.* New York: Gloucester Press, 1993.

Smoothey, Marion. *Area and Volume.* New York: Marshall Cavendish, 1992.

———. *Estimating.* New York: Marshall Cavendish, 1994.

Walpole, Brenda. *Distance.* Milwaukee: Gareth Stevens, 1995.

———. *Speed.* Milwaukee: Gareth Stevens, 1995.

Internet Addresses

Charischak, Ihor. "Measuring Heights." February 1996. <http://forum.swarthmore.edu/~ihor/trig.htm/> (July 8, 1999).

Energy Quest. "Measuring the Wind." *Energy and Science Projects for Students.* n.d. <http://www.energy.ca.gov/education/projects/projects-html/windmeasure.html> (July 8, 1999).

Index